J B Reagan
Marsico, Katie
Ronald Reagan

SM

$34.21
ocn458892735
09/22/2011

RONALD REAGAN

The Presidents of the United States

George Washington
1789–1797

John Adams
1797–1801

Thomas Jefferson
1801–1809

James Madison
1809–1817

James Monroe
1817–1825

John Quincy Adams
1825–1829

Andrew Jackson
1829–1837

Martin Van Buren
1837–1841

William Henry Harrison
1841

John Tyler
1841–1845

James Polk
1845–1849

Zachary Taylor
1849–1850

Millard Fillmore
1850–1853

Franklin Pierce
1853–1857

James Buchanan
1857–1861

Abraham Lincoln
1861–1865

Andrew Johnson
1865–1869

Ulysses S. Grant
1869–1877

Rutherford B. Hayes
1877–1881

James Garfield
1881

Chester Arthur
1881–1885

Grover Cleveland
1885–1889

Benjamin Harrison
1889–1893

Grover Cleveland
1893–1897

William McKinley
1897–1901

Theodore Roosevelt
1901–1909

William H. Taft
1909–1913

Woodrow Wilson
1913–1921

Warren Harding
1921–1923

Calvin Coolidge
1923–1929

Herbert Hoover
1929–1933

Franklin D. Roosevelt
1933–1945

Harry Truman
1945–1953

Dwight Eisenhower
1953–1961

John F. Kennedy
1961–1963

Lyndon B. Johnson
1963–1969

Richard Nixon
1969–1974

Gerald Ford
1974–1977

Jimmy Carter
1977–1981

Ronald Reagan
1981–1989

George H. W. Bush
1989–1993

William J. Clinton
1993–2001

George W. Bush
2001–2009

Barack Obama
2009–

RONALD REAGAN

KATIE MARSICO

Marshall Cavendish
Benchmark
New York

Published by Marshall Cavendish Benchmark
An imprint of Marshall Cavendish Corporation

Website: www.marshallcavendish.us

Other Marshall Cavendish Offices:
Marshall Cavendish International (Asia) Private Limited, 1 New Industrial Road, Singapore 536196 •
Marshall Cavendish International (Thailand) Co Ltd. 253 Asoke, 12th Flr, Sukhumvit 21 Road, Klongtoey
Nua, Wattana, Bangkok 10110, Thailand • Marshall Cavendish (Malaysia) Sdn Bhd, Times Subang, Lot
46, Subang Hi-Tech Industrial Park, Batu Tiga, 40000 Shah Alam, Selangor Darul Ehsan, Malaysia

Marshall Cavendish is a trademark of Times Publishing Limited

All websites were available and accurate when this book was sent to press.

Library of Congress Cataloging-in-Publication Data

Marsico, Katie, 1980–
Ronald Reagan / by Katie Marsico.
p. cm.—(Presidents and their times)
Summary: "Provides comprehensive information on President Ronald Reagan and places him within his
historical and cultural context. Also explored are the formative events of his times and how he
responded"—Provided by publisher.
Includes bibliographical references and index.
ISBN 978-0-7614-4814-3
1. Reagan, Ronald—Juvenile literature.
2. Presidents—United States—Biography—Juvenile literature. I. Title.
E877.M365 2011
973.927092—dc22
[B]
2009044590

Editor: Christine Florie
Publisher: Michelle Bisson
Art Director: Anahid Hamparian
Series Designer: Alex Ferrari

Photo research by Thomas Khoo

The photographs in this book are used by permission and through the courtesy of: *Alamy:* 23, 48;
alt.type/Reuters: 88, 89, 90, 95 (r); *Corbis:* 6, 9, 11, 12, 13, 18, 20, 24, 30, 31, 33, 34, 40, 42, 51, 54, 59,
61, 67, 69, 72, 74, 78, 82, 86, 94 (l & r), 95 (l); *Getty Images:* 66, 76, 77; *Photolibrary:* 27; *Topfoto:*
cover, 3, 39, 45, 53, 56, 63, 70, 93.

Printed in Malaysia
1 3 5 6 4 2

CONTENTS

ONE   *Early Life of a Future Leader*   7

TWO   *Radio Announcer and Rising Star*   16

THREE   *Pathways to a Political Career*   26

FOUR   *The Respected Republican*   36

FIVE   *From California to the Nation's Capital*   47

SIX   *Winning and Working in the White House*   58

SEVEN   *The Rough Road to a Better Tomorrow*   71

EIGHT   *Final Years of the Fortieth President*   84

TIMELINE   94

NOTES   96

GLOSSARY   99

FURTHER INFORMATION   101

BIBLIOGRAPHY   103

INDEX   107

★ ★ ★ ★ ★ ★ ★ ★ ★ ★ ★ ★ ★ ★ ★

In addition to serving as America's fortieth president, Reagan was known for being an engaging public speaker.

EARLY LIFE OF A FUTURE LEADER

Ronald Wilson Reagan, America's fortieth president, once said, "To sit back, hoping that someday, some way, someone will make things right is to go on feeding the crocodile, hoping he will eat you last—but eat you he will." From his perspective, it was important for U.S. citizens to push forward, fighting for progress and protecting the rights and freedoms they had enjoyed for more than two hundred years. As president, Reagan considered it his responsibility to see to it that they accomplished such goals.

He led the nation from 1981 to 1989—an era when the country was experiencing a variety of both exciting and terrifying changes. Yet the man who began life as a small-town boy in Illinois did not always have ambitions to pursue a career in politics. Reagan had gradually made his way from acting in films to winning the governorship of California in the 1960s.

By the time he entered the White House in the early 1980s, he was faced with challenges ranging from economic crises to international **terrorism.** The manner in which he dealt with these situations sometimes earned him praise. Reagan was nicknamed the Great Communicator for his ability to speak to both average Americans and foreign heads of state with ease and eloquence. Many people felt they connected with him and that he understood and cared about their problems.

On the other hand, Reagan's critics often accused him of allowing his aides to handle matters that he should have decided himself. They argued that he put forth real effort as a leader only when he was promoting issues that appealed to him personally, such as combating communism and strengthening national defenses. In addition, several of his opponents believed that he mismanaged **diplomatic** relations in the Middle East and other parts of the globe.

Despite the different views people have of Reagan, most agree that his leadership and its legacy will not be forgotten anytime soon. He served the United States during a remarkable chapter in its history. Both his errors and achievements reshaped a country for generations to come.

GROWING UP IN ILLINOIS

Ronald Reagan was born on February 6, 1911, in the town of Tampico, Illinois, in a one-bedroom apartment on the second floor of a bank building. Tampico, located a little more than 100 miles west of Chicago, Illinois, and the shores of Lake Michigan, was a small and peaceful community. Reagan's father, John Edward "Jack" Reagan, was of Irish ancestry. His mother, Nelle Wilson, was Scottish and English. Reagan also had a brother, Neil, who was two years older.

Though Ronald began life in Tampico, that Illinois town would not be the only one in which he resided during his childhood. His father, who worked as a salesman and a store clerk, frequently uprooted the family as he transitioned from one job to another. Jack Reagan was a handsome, charming man whom Ronald would always remember with affection. Unfortunately, he was also plagued by a severe drinking problem.

Nelle supported her husband as he struggled with alcoholism and his many career changes. When she was not tending to the

This early portrait shows Ronald (third from left) and his parents and brother. The Reagans experienced their share of hardship but were a loving, close-knit family.

Ronald "Dutch" Reagan

Not long after Ronald was born, his father gave him the nickname "Dutch." When Jack got a look at his youngest son—who weighed about 10 pounds at birth—he supposedly remarked that he resembled "a fat Dutchman." The name stuck for the rest of Ronald's life, though it was most popular during his boyhood. He even encouraged friends and family to call him Dutch because he believed it sounded more masculine than "Ronald."

needs of her family, she donated her time to functions sponsored by the Disciples of Christ Church, of which she was an active member. Her husband, on the other hand, was Roman Catholic. These different spiritual beliefs resulted in Neil being brought up in Jack's faith and Ronald being raised according to Nelle's. Despite not sharing the same religion as his father and brother and having to cope with issues such as alcoholism and the family's frequent moves, Ronald described his childhood as relatively happy.

"I learned from my father the value of hard work and ambition, and maybe a little something about telling a story," he later recalled in an autobiography. "From my mother, I learned the value of prayer, how to have dreams and believe I could make them come true." This attitude helped young Ronald adapt to life in each of the Illinois towns he ultimately called home. During his childhood, his family resided in Tampico, Dixon, Galesburg, and Monmouth, as well as the city of Chicago. Finally, when

Ronald was nine, they returned to Dixon, where he spent his adolescence.

While enrolled in Dixon's school system, he enjoyed participating in sports such as football and swimming. Ronald was also heavily involved in school dramatic productions, which foreshadowed a future that would be shaped by his speaking and performing abilities. He was an average student, but he proved that he had an exceptional memory and used it to his advantage when studying at the last minute for tests and exams. In addition, Ronald was a hard worker and, as a teen, spent summers employed as a lifeguard at a local beach.

Although Ronald seemed to adjust to the instability that sometimes characterized his youth, he still experienced challenges in certain areas. For example, Ronald was popular and got along with most of his peers, but he later confessed that he had trouble getting close to the friends he made. Moving so often may have impacted his ability to form deeper relationships that required a greater level of trust and commitment. Not

Ronald played on several varsity sports teams during his years at Dixon High School.

Reagan did not have the luxury of relaxing during his breaks from school. He instead began building his savings by working as a lifeguard.

helping matters was his father's sense of pessimism, or the attitude that things will always turn out badly.

Ronald tended to be more hopeful, or optimistic. By the time he graduated from high school in 1928, he had managed to earn a partial sports scholarship to Eureka College in Eureka, Illinois. He planned to supplement his educational expenses with money he had set aside from his work as a lifeguard. Looking forward to the future that lay ahead of him, he wrote in his 1928 yearbook, "Life is just one grand, sweet song, so start the music."

INTERESTS AND AMBITIONS OF THE COLLEGE BOY

The mere fact that Reagan was attending college was an accomplishment, especially considering that fewer than 10 percent of his high school classmates in Dixon could boast that they were doing the same. Nevertheless, he did not appear overly eager to distinguish himself academically at Eureka. His grades were generally unimpressive, and his brother and teachers later noted that he passed courses by using his "photographic mind" to memorize lessons shortly before exams. Yet Reagan proved popular with his fellow students and demonstrated his skills as an actor and public speaker by participating in the college's drama society.

While he may have been somewhat lazy when it came to his studies, he worked hard to support himself financially. Reagan held various jobs washing dishes and serving food in dining halls and fraternity houses on campus. When he was not looking for new ways to earn money, he took part in student government and contributed to Eureka's newspaper and yearbook. He also played football and was a member of the varsity swim team.

Reagan continued to participate in athletics while in college. Here he is shown preparing to dive for Eureka's swim team.

Reagan was fascinated by student politics as well. Even as a freshman, he readily stepped up to the podium and spoke out against cutbacks authorized by Eureka's administration. In order to slash the school budget, the college president laid off professors and eliminated classes that many students needed to take to graduate. Reagan played an active role in the student strike that followed in the autumn of 1928 and made an impact on his peers by delivering a stirring speech protesting the cutbacks. Eureka's president eventually resigned in response to such opposition.

The event was not insignificant for Reagan. The eloquent young college student had known for a while that he was an effective public speaker. Yet he suddenly got a firsthand look at how he could use his abilities to influence people around him and to fight for changes that he considered important.

"Giving that speech—my first—was as exciting as any I ever gave," Reagan later remembered. "For the first time in my life, I felt my words reach out and grab an audience, and it was exhilarating. When I'd say something . . . it was as if the audience and I were one. When I called for a vote on the strike, everybody rose to their feet with a thunderous clapping of hands and approved the proposal."

When Reagan graduated from Eureka on June 4, 1932, however, there was little indication that this experience inspired him to pursue a career in politics. He had earned a degree in sociology and economics, but this achievement was no guarantee that he would find work after leaving school. Starting in 1929, America had descended into an economic crisis known as the Great Depression.

After the stock market crashed in October of that year, people across the country lost their businesses, jobs, and homes.

Family fortunes disappeared practically overnight, and U.S. citizens stood in crowded breadlines just to get a meal. By the time Reagan received his diploma from Eureka in the summer of 1932, one in four Americans was unemployed, and his job prospects appeared limited.

His father, who had recently owned a shoe shop, lost his business, prompting Nelle to take up work as a seamstress. The family had no choice but to sublet most of the home they had been renting in Dixon and live out of a single room. Reagan had wanted to become a radio announcer after graduation, but accomplishing that career goal seemed less and less likely every time he visited a station in the Illinois area, looking for work.

The ambitious young man hitchhiked to Chicago in 1932, hoping to find work there. However, with the nation in the grips of an economic crisis, no one was hiring. The situation in Dixon was not much better. The public park where Reagan had previously served as a lifeguard closed for the summer, eliminating what he considered his remaining chance of employment in his hometown. Despite the odds stacked against him, however, the twenty-one-year-old was determined to find a job—and preferably at a radio station. As Reagan would discover in the months ahead and throughout the remainder of his life, such persistence inevitably pays off.

RADIO ANNOUNCER AND RISING STAR

$\mathcal{I}$n the fall of 1932 Reagan's luck finally began to change. After being turned away by a program director at WOC Radio in Davenport, Iowa, he prepared to leave yet another station unsuccessful and unemployed. This time, however, Reagan could not help but express his frustration for everyone around him to hear.

"How," he wondered aloud as he headed for the elevator, "do you get to be a sports announcer if you can't get a [job at a radio] station?" Apparently, the program director considered the question a good one and was impressed by what he saw. Despite having interviewed several candidates the previous day, he allowed Reagan to audition by providing an improvised account of a college football game. The request was by no means simple—he had to sound as excited as if he were covering a live sporting event and as unhesitating as if it were unfolding before his very eyes. Fortunately for Reagan, the photographic memory that had enabled him to glide through courses at Eureka also helped him to recollect a game he had played there in great detail.

It was enough to win him temporary work at WOC, broadcasting a few college sporting events. Yet his employment status was shaky. Once football season concluded that year, the station informed him that they no longer had any need for his services but would keep him in mind if something else came along. It inevitably did, and WOC called Reagan in February 1933 to let him know that a staff announcer had quit, leaving an opening that paid one hundred dollars a month.

"As staff announcer, I played phonograph records, read commercials, and served as a vocal bridge between our local programming and network broadcasts," Reagan later recalled. "I was not an immediate success as a radio announcer, to put it mildly. Nobody had bothered to give me any instructions . . . and I quickly proved it on the air. I stumbled over my words and had a delivery as wooden as a prairie oak."

This was especially true when it came to reading scripted commercials. In fact, sponsors were so dissatisfied with his performance that the station made plans to fire him. Reagan—who was expected to train his replacement—scared the young man off by making it seem like WOC offered no job stability. Ultimately, he kept his job there and convinced the program director to coach him on improving his broadcasting skills.

Reagan's hard work helped advance his career. In May 1933 he moved to Des Moines, Iowa, to join the staff of WOC's larger sister station, WHO. Reagan's abilities soon earned him a reputation as one of the Midwest's best sports broadcasters. This was no small achievement in the 1930s, before the days of television. Many people considered radio the best way to receive the most up-to-date information about everything from world affairs to football games.

After less than a year on the air, Reagan had managed to develop a career for himself at the forefront of regional broadcasting. Yet, despite his success at WHO, he had other ambitions that stretched back to his days as a member of Eureka's drama society. As time passed, he began focusing on making it big as an actor in sunny Hollywood, California.

Reagan eventually built a name for himself as a broadcaster, but it took time to develop his skills on the air and to convince radio bosses he was well suited to the job.

HEADED TO HOLLYWOOD

Just as determined to pursue the career he now envisioned for himself as he had been about becoming a radio announcer in 1932, Reagan strategized about making it to Hollywood. In 1937 he cleverly convinced WHO to send him to California to cover the Chicago Cubs' spring training on Catalina Island. Once on the Pacific Coast, however, Reagan did not confine himself to stadium benches. Instead, he wasted no time in looking up Joy

Hodges, a former WHO employee who had moved to California. She was in the process of developing her career as a singer and actress. Hodges helped Reagan get his foot in the door with her agent, who, like the program director at WOC five years earlier, was impressed by what he saw.

The agent called Warner Brothers, a major Hollywood movie studio, and claimed that he had "another Robert Taylor" sitting in his office. Taylor was regarded as one of the industry's most dashing, talented stars, and the comparison landed Reagan a screen test. Studio representatives told him to stay in Los Angeles, California, for a few more days while they decided if they wanted to offer him a contract. Much to their surprise, Reagan refused to

SHARING SUCCESS

Even after he moved away from home, Reagan continued to maintain close family ties and tried to support his parents and brother. From his perspective, he had achieved career stability and financial security during an era when few Americans could boast the same. It was important to him to share his success with loved ones back in Illinois, especially since Jack, Nelle, and Neil Reagan had been hit hard by the effects of the Great Depression.

"I'd accomplished my goal and enjoyed every minute of it," he recollected. "Before long, during the depths of the Depression, I was earning seventy-five dollars a week and gaining the kind of fame in the Midwest that brought in invitations for speaking engagements that provided extra income I could use to help out my parents."

remain in the area, noting that he had a commitment to his current employers as a broadcaster back in Iowa.

Many people would have gladly waited more than a few days if it meant the possibility of a job with Warner Brothers. Reagan, however, was unwilling to simply abandon his responsibilities at WHO for an uncertain future in California. He had dreams of becoming an actor, but he also grasped that the country was still reeling from the effects of the Great Depression. He therefore had to weigh the risk of losing steady work at a radio station that paid a decent salary against the possibility of advancing his career in Hollywood.

Studio executives believed Reagan's handsome looks and engaging manner would win the approval of movie audiences.

Luckily for Reagan, he did not lose the gamble he took when he returned to Des Moines in the spring of 1937. Shortly after he got back, he received a telegram from the agent who had interviewed him. Warner Brothers wanted to offer Reagan a seven-year contract that promised to pay two hundred dollars a week. Given the times and the economic situation that was overwhelming so many Americans in the 1930s, the job security and pay represented remarkable success for a young man who had barely turned twenty-six.

Reagan responded to the telegram by ordering the agent to accept the offer before Warner Brothers changed its mind. He then resigned from WHO and started preparing for his move to Los Angeles in the late spring of 1937. Yet, regardless of how confident Reagan had learned to seem as he broadcast sports games on the radio or interviewed with Hollywood casting directors, he was humbled by the career transition that lay ahead of him.

"On a Monday morning," he recalled in his subsequent autobiography, "in the first week of June in 1937, I drove my convertible through the gates of the Warner Brothers lot in Burbank, ready for work, and with a hole in my stomach as deep as an oil well. I asked myself, 'what am *I* doing here?'" As nervous as Reagan might have felt, however, Hollywood was prepared to help him answer that question.

MOUNTING SUCCESS IN THE MOVIES

The new actor from Dixon, Illinois, may have found his way onto a Warner Brothers lot, but that did not mean he was an instant movie star. At first Reagan either landed smaller parts in major motion pictures or played leading roles in B movies. Films that fall into this latter category generally involve low production costs and limited acclaim.

Despite the fact that Reagan did not immediately skyrocket to the top of show business, he earned a reputation on movie sets as being likable, cooperative, and professional. He used his sharp memory to recite dialogue exactly as it was written and just as directors wanted it read. Reagan's dedication and overall personality made him appealing to work with, as Hollywood starlet Jane Wyman discovered in 1939 when the pair filmed *Brother Rat.*

The movie—which was his ninth since moving to California—tells the story of students attending the Virginia Military Institute (VMI) in Lexington, Virginia. It was the most significant role Reagan had played in a major motion picture up to that point. Just as important, though, it served as the setting in which he and Jane fell in love. She was going through a divorce, but that did not stop the couple from announcing their engagement before production on *Brother Rat* drew to a close. On January 24, 1940, Reagan and Jane were married. Their daughter, Maureen Elizabeth, was born in January 1941.

The early 1940s proved an exciting period in Reagan's life for other reasons as well. At Jane's urging, he became more aggressive about seeking out larger parts in bigger-budget films. He therefore pushed studio executives at Warner Brothers to cast him as college football hero George Gipp in the 1940 flick *Knute Rockne—All American*. Despite their reluctance due to the fact that Reagan was not a blockbuster star, the studio executives granted his wish.

The movie, which recounts the career of football coach Knute Rockne at Notre Dame University in South Bend, Indiana, also depicts the achievements of Gipp, who was one of the college's athletic stars. Sadly, the young player died at an early age due to pneumonia. While portraying Gipp on his deathbed, Reagan utters the following famous line to Rockne's character: "Some day when things are tough, maybe you can ask the boys to go in there and win just one for the Gipper." Though *Knute Rockne—All American* premiered in 1940, the well-known phrase and the nickname "Gipper" remained attached to the actor for decades to come. In fact, reporters frequently made references to these expressions during Reagan's political campaigns.

Though they appeared to be the perfect couple in this portrait, Reagan and Jane were destined to experience a strained and often unhappy relationship.

The role of Gipp was the most famous Reagan would play as a Hollywood star.

As of the early 1940s, however, Reagan was not considering running for political office. He was enjoying family life with Jane and their daughter, as well as the praise and recognition he earned for *Knute Rockne—All American.* Critics applauded his portrayal of Gipp, and studio executives at Warner Brothers responded by giving him meatier roles in bigger-budget productions. *Kings Row,* which was released in 1941, and *Desperate Journey,* which opened the following year, are two examples of such films.

From Reagan's perspective, many of his dreams were finally coming true against the backdrop of Hollywood. Yet, just as he appeared to be on a steady climb upward in terms of career accomplishments and overall success, he was forced to cope with a series of unexpected challenges. War, personal tragedy, and new ambitions would reshape his existence as the decade wore on.

Pathways to a Political Career

While Reagan was busy starting a family and building his film career, World War II (1939–1945) erupted in Europe and island nations of the Pacific Ocean. During the course of this conflict, nations including Great Britain, the United States, and the Soviet Union banded together to form the Allied powers. They battled the Axis powers, which consisted of Germany, Italy, Japan, and other countries. Not all of these nations became involved in World War II right away, though. While the United States frowned upon Axis leaders launching invasions throughout Europe and the Pacific, it managed to remain relatively neutral until December 7, 1941. On that date Japan organized an air attack on Pearl Harbor, a naval base on the Hawaiian island of Oahu. U.S. president Franklin Roosevelt responded by asking Congress to declare war on Japan. It was not long before millions of American troops were called to fight the Axis powers.

Though many were sent overseas, some were allowed to remain on the home front. Reagan, who was a member of the army **reserve**, was among this second group. His nearsightedness prevented him from being assigned to combat. Warner Brothers also lobbied the government to keep him in the United States to fulfill his filming commitments. At first studio executives persuaded the U.S. military to defer, or postpone, his service by claiming that Reagan was busy shooting movies with patriotic themes that would strengthen Americans' support for the war.

When he at last reported for duty in the spring of 1942, the army assigned him to California bases. Much of his service took place in Culver City, California, which is about 10 miles from Warner Brothers Studios and was close to Jane Wyman and their daughter, Maureen. Reagan spent most of his time making training films for the U.S. Air Force. Though Warner Brothers depicted him in newsreels as a soldier who frequently had to leave his family to participate in the war effort, he was rarely far from home.

Unlike many U.S. servicemen, Reagan did not have to endure any major separation from his family during World War II.

Yet Reagan paid a price for his service all the same. Prior to U.S. involvement in World War II, his career as a Hollywood star was starting to flourish. Thanks to his acclaimed performance in *Knute Rockne—All American*, he was getting bigger parts in better movies. When the war ended and the U.S. military finally discharged Reagan in July 1945, however, his climb to stardom seemed to stall. He was eager to play meaningful dramatic roles, but Warner Brothers was inclined to cast him in lighthearted, comedic roles.

As Reagan became increasingly frustrated with his return to bit parts and B movies, he also faced troubles at home. Though his career appeared to be at a standstill, Jane's continued to grow, as did their family. The couple had adopted a baby boy named Michael Edward in early 1945 and were expecting again by the beginning of 1947. Tragically, Reagan's second child with Jane survived only one day after being born four months premature in June of that year. The stress surrounding this loss, as well as tensions related to differences in their career paths, led them to divorce in 1949.

Leading a Union Amidst Fears of Communism

Though Reagan may have experienced loneliness when his marriage ended, he certainly was not left with too much time on his hands. The actor was disappointed at the new selection of roles that Warner Brothers encouraged him to take, but he was nevertheless building a name for himself as an active member of the film industry. This was partially a result of his leadership efforts within the Screen Actors Guild (SAG).

SAG is a labor **union** that was formed in 1933 to help protect actors' rights. As such, it attempts to ensure that performers receive adequate compensation and benefits in exchange for their services. SAG also monitors contract negotiations with production studios. Reagan had joined the organization not long after he arrived in California in 1937. By July 1941 he had been appointed to the union's board. In 1947 he was elected the president of SAG and would continue to hold that office for five consecutive terms.

"As I look back now," Reagan later reflected, "I guess I was . . . beginning a political transformation that was born in an off-screen cauldron of deceit and subversion and a personal journey of discovery that would leave me with a growing distaste for big government. I didn't realize it, but I'd started on a path that was going to lead me a long way from Hollywood." There is no doubt that heading SAG required him to develop his skills as a negotiator. In addition, Reagan often found himself dealing with intense political controversies that extended far beyond salary disputes and the fine print in studio contracts.

Starting in the mid–1940s, many Americans were gripped by a fear of communism. This political philosophy supports the idea of a classless society where everyone shares common ownership of property and businesses. In communist nations the state controls the economy—and often several other aspects of peoples' day-to-day lives. Communist governments are frequently regarded as oppressive and restrictive when it comes to citizens' rights.

Communism is not practiced in the United States, where people believe in **democracy** and capitalism, or private ownership. It was, however, the accepted political system within the Soviet Union. While that nation had fought alongside America during World War II, the two shared a hostile relationship starting in about 1945. Known as the cold war (1945–1991), it lasted several decades but did not feature outright military combat between U.S. citizens and the Soviets.

It instead included heated technological and military competition, spy tactics, and numerous **propaganda** campaigns. Tension also arose when each nation periodically backed the other's enemies in warfare that broke out in countries like Korea, Vietnam, and Afghanistan. And, because the Soviet Union was rooted in communism, Americans worried about the spread of this political philosophy throughout the United States. They were alarmed at the idea of communists influencing everyone from U.S. politicians to military leaders to Hollywood actors and directors.

This political cartoon depicts a Russian communist soldier (right) scolding a U.S. serviceman. Some Americans worried that such propaganda would influence Americans' ways of thinking

As a result of this paranoia many citizens who worked for or were connected to the government were forced to swear oaths of loyalty. Some were even questioned by the House Committee on Un-American Activities (HUAC). This congressional group had been created in 1938 to investigate allegations of treason and **subversion.** As Reagan discovered during his leadership of SAG, officials serving on the committee gradually began turning their attention to the threat of communism within the motion picture industry.

HOLLYWOOD BLACKLISTS AND NEW BEGINNINGS

Congressmen who served on the HUAC were suspicious of actors, directors, writers, and producers who had communist beliefs or expressed sympathy for the Soviet Union. They eventually held hearings and called several witnesses—including Reagan—to testify about any subversive influences in Hollywood. As the president of SAG, Reagan did not believe that communists had gained control of American filmmaking. Nor did he necessarily approve of what he perceived as the HUAC's attempts to bully and intimidate the men and women it called upon to testify.

At the same time, however, Reagan was a firm anticommunist. Ultimately, it appears that he had mixed feelings about studio executives' decision to **blacklist** those Hollywood writers and directors that the HUAC determined were members of the Communist Party.

Reagan was called to testify before the HUAC in 1947 at a time in American history when fears of communism gripped the nation.

Some of these individuals were sent to prison, fined, and refused work in American motion pictures. Many were even forced to use pseudonyms, or false names, to obtain employment.

To this day, historians debate Reagan's opinion of blacklisting. Certain biographers allege that he supported the practice because he recognized how the political opinions of anyone associated with a film could shape audiences' attitudes toward it. Others insist that he opposed the blacklist and worked to help those Hollywood professionals whose reputations had been ruined because of it.

Regardless of his true thoughts on the subject, however, the blacklist is what led him to meet his second wife in late 1949. That year, an acquaintance of his called and asked him to use his influence to aid the young actress Nancy Davis. In a case of mistaken identity, she was being incorrectly labeled as a communist sympathizer.

Reagan and Nancy agreed to meet for dinner to discuss the situation, and what followed was a romance that resulted in a wedding on March 4, 1952. Unlike Jane, she quickly abandoned her career after she got married. By October 1952 the couple welcomed their first child, Patricia "Patti" Ann. A son named Ronald Prescott arrived in May 1958.

As Reagan built his new life with Nancy and their children in California, he also started reshaping his career. The same year they had Patti, he gave up his presidency of SAG. Disappointed in the limited roles Warner Brothers offered him after World War II, he had signed a contract in 1949 that allowed him to work with other studios. Unfortunately, the move did little to revive the career growth he had experienced before fighting erupted.

*Reagan began a
fifty-two-year
marriage with
Nancy in
March 1952.*

THE ROLE OF REAGAN'S SECOND WIFE

Though she gave up her own Hollywood career shortly after getting married in 1952, Nancy was far more than a wife and mother. Reagan frequently relied on her opinions when it came to addressing important political issues. In fact, his critics eventually complained that he allowed Nancy too great a voice in matters of state. They noted that she had an incredible influence on everything from his scheduled public appearances to which politicians made up Reagan's inner circle of advisers.

For her part, Nancy admitted that she was committed to her husband and his career. Yet she also argued that people overemphasized her impact on how the government was run. In addition, she explained that while she and Reagan loved each other, she sometimes found him to be emotionally distant.

"He often seems remote," she observed, "and he doesn't let anybody get too close. There's a wall around him. He lets me come closer than anyone else, but there are times when even I feel that barrier."

In 1954 Reagan therefore eagerly accepted the opportunity to host a television drama known as *General Electric Theater*. The job required him to both act on the show and tour various plants and corporate offices owned by the appliance company General Electric (GE). While serving as president of SAG had introduced Reagan to the ins and outs of politics, working for GE provided him with added opportunities to give speeches and interact with the public.

"I think everybody expected me to get up and tell a few Hollywood stories as usual and then sit down," he recalled of his days touring GE facilities. "But instead, I decided to give a speech about the pride of giving and the importance of doing things without waiting for the government to do it for you." He added, "Those GE tours became almost a postgraduate course in political science for me. I was seeing how government really operated and affected people in America, not how it was taught in school." Sometimes making up to fourteen speeches a day, Reagan started to openly express political views that opposed federal **regulation** of business and supported the rights of large corporations. It would not be long before he was well known for these opinions—as well as for having the potential to become a politician.

THE RESPECTED REPUBLICAN

The political views Reagan developed while working for GE were not the same ones he had held for most of his life. The ideas of restricting government regulation of businesses and protecting the rights of larger corporations are generally considered Republican values. Starting in about 1932, however, Reagan had voiced his support of Democratic politicians, including presidents Franklin Roosevelt and Harry Truman.

The Democrats make up America's other major political party. Unlike Republicans, Democrats of this era generally supported the government's right to regulate economic activity. They believed strong federal control was necessary in order to prevent **monopolies** from forming and to help smaller businesses develop and survive.

Yet, by the time Reagan was employed at GE, his political opinions tended to be less in keeping with those of the Democratic Party. By 1960 Reagan had decided that he was against that party's ideas—as well as the thought of the young Democratic presidential candidate John Kennedy winning that year's election. He therefore campaigned in favor of Republican nominee Richard Nixon. Though Kennedy beat his opponent and made his way to the White House in January 1961, Reagan only increased his displays of loyalty to the Republicans. In 1962 he officially became a registered member of the Republican Party.

Reagan frequently voiced his ideals when he toured for GE, which led some officials to urge him to tone down the political nature of his speeches. As of 1962, though, this would become somewhat of a nonissue. That year, slipping ratings led GE to cancel *General Electric Theater.*

Reagan found new work as the host of a television western called *Death Valley Days.* Yet he was also starting to consider extending his career beyond the confines of acting. Ever since he had headed SAG in the 1940s, he had been exposed to politics and their influence on day-to-day life. Despite his not having any actual experience in government, the fact that he was an established film and television personality prompted people to listen when he delivered a speech or expressed his views. And, like any well-trained actor, Reagan knew how to appeal to his audience.

He often used his sense of humor to lighten the atmosphere, and his tours with GE had taught him how to talk *with* members of the public, as opposed to simply speaking *to* them. He was skilled at engaging crowds in a charming, lighthearted manner. At the same time, though, Reagan was also capable of tackling serious subjects and was passionate in his opposition to communism and government regulation of businesses.

His personality may have seemed mild, but his political opinions were far from **moderate.** In fact, they appealed to right-wing Republicans, or more **conservative** members of that political party. Beginning in the early 1960s, such individuals began to perceive Reagan as a potentially valuable spokesperson whom they hoped to use to win back the White House in 1964.

Gaining Recognition in the Goldwater Campaign

Four years after Kennedy had been elected president, Republicans were eager to regain political control of that office. Many saw candidate Barry Goldwater as a means of accomplishing this goal. They realized, though, that he was up against stiff competition. When Kennedy was assassinated, or murdered, in November 1963, Vice President Lyndon Johnson had been sworn in as leader of the nation.

Hoping to secure additional time in the White House in 1964, Johnson proved a difficult opponent for Goldwater to overcome. One of the main controversies that would impact Johnson's political career—American involvement in the Vietnam War (1954–1975)—had not yet gained intensity. In addition, the U.S. economy was flourishing at that point in history, and a great number of people sympathized with the president and the Democratic Party in general because of Kennedy's tragic death.

Meanwhile, Goldwater faced division within the Republican camp. More moderate party members were against his extremely conservative views. For all of these reasons, he was slumping in the polls and looked to Reagan, with whom he had been acquainted for several years, to help boost his campaign. The fifty-three-year-old actor answered Goldwater's call for support and built his own political career in the process.

On October 27, 1964, Reagan delivered a famous televised speech titled "A Time for Choosing." While it was intended to drum up votes for Goldwater, it was more successful in crafting his own image as an eloquent and educated newcomer on America's political scene. Audiences across the country were

Reagan started crafting his public image as a serious Republican politician during his campaign efforts for Goldwater (shown here) in 1964.

Reagan demonstrated his support of Goldwater in 1964. In some camps, though, the campaign became just as much about winning the new Hollywood Republican recognition as it was about fighting for Goldwater himself.

impressed by his message to U.S. citizens, which essentially challenged them to vote for the candidate whom they believed would best protect the nation for generations to come.

"You and I have a rendezvous with destiny," Reagan declared to television cameras in 1964. "We will preserve for our children this last best hope of man on earth or we will sentence them to take the first step into a thousand years of darkness. If we fail, at least let our children, and our children's children, say of us we justified our brief moment here. We did all that could be done."

Although the speech earned Reagan widespread political recognition, it was not enough to propel Goldwater to the White House. In November 1964 Johnson swept the polls, claiming about 61 percent of the popular vote and the backing of 486 members of the **Electoral College**. Goldwater, on the other hand, earned less than 39 percent of the ballots cast on election day. Within the Electoral College only fifty-two electors offered him their support.

Goldwater would continue to enjoy a political career as a U.S. senator, but many conservative Republicans began looking toward Reagan as a future leader. In early 1965 several successful California businessmen who were also well-known members of the Republican Party gathered to discuss the state governorship. They needed a strong candidate to prevent the current politician in that office, Democrat Edmund "Pat" Brown, from winning a third term.

Local Republicans decided Reagan was the man for the job, but he was not completely convinced that they were correct. He had certainly made a fair number of public speeches to endorse

At first, Brown (shown here) had few worries that he would easily clinch victory from the politically inexperienced Reagan.

various candidates and ideas, but he had never held an official government job. Ultimately, however, his interest in politics and the insistence of right-wing Republicans that he run for governor outweighed any reluctance he had. Before formally entering the race, though, he first consulted with Nancy—and came to terms with how a political career would drastically reshape their existence.

"If I decided to run, we agreed our life we knew and loved would change dramatically, perhaps forever," Reagan later recalled. "But I told Nancy: 'I don't think we can run away from it.' She agreed . . . and on a television broadcast [on] January 4, 1966, I announced my intention to seek the Republican nomination for governor."

Voted into the Lions' Den

Though his fellow Republicans may have been impressed by Reagan as he prepared to fight for the governorship of California in 1966, Brown was far from awestruck. He thought the idea of running against an actor with no prior political experience was laughable. After the former film star won the Republican **primary,** however, Brown discovered exactly how wrong he had been to underestimate his opponent.

Only an Actor?

One of Brown's most famous criticisms of his opponent was, "Reagan is only an actor who memorizes speeches written by other people, just like he memorized the lines that were fed to him by his screenwriters in the movies. Sure, he makes a good speech, but who's *writing* his speeches?" Reagan felt the best way to combat the idea that he was not able to think for himself was to encourage question-and-answer sessions with members of the public along his campaign trail.

Initially, not all of his advisers thought this was wise, especially since it could potentially result in his being caught off guard on a variety of political topics. They were quickly reassured, however, when they witnessed Reagan's ability to interact with voters. Apart from proving that he was knowledgeable about current affairs, the question-and-answer platform also helped him find out what subjects the public considered important. As Reagan noted, it "turned out to be a wonderful way to learn about the issues that were on people's minds."

Reagan's supporters responded to the governor's criticisms by proclaiming that, while a newcomer, their candidate was more dedicated to serving the interests of average people because he was just that—an average person. The fact that he lacked significant political experience also meant that he had not been exposed to corrupt government practices. Californians who wanted to see Reagan elected argued that he was more in tune with the needs of citizens than Brown and would therefore do a more efficient job when running the state.

Such individuals pointed to events at the University of California–Berkeley to back up this claim. As an increasing number of American soldiers began streaming into Asia to fight the Vietnam War, protests and riots over U.S. involvement erupted across the nation. The Asian conflict essentially pitted communist forces in North Vietnam against South Vietnamese troops, who were reinforced by American soldiers.

Yet not everyone agreed with the United States' presence in South Asia. Numerous student groups opposed the military draft that was taking place. Other activists insisted that America should never have become entangled in another country's war and accused the government of trying to rule Vietnam. Student demonstrations, including those that rocked Berkeley, frequently turned disruptive and violent.

Reagan lashed back at Brown's attacks on his inexperience by telling voters that the governor should have been more forceful in stamping out campus unrest. He promised that, unlike his opponent, he would restore order and efficiency to California and would push to reduce the state's high taxes. Reagan vowed to change the governorship for the better, and he did so in a way that captivated the public.

As he traveled throughout the state and gave numerous speeches, he engaged the crowds who showed up to hear him talk. He encouraged voters to ask questions and used humor and charm to respond to them in a manner that they could relate to. In the end the Great Communicator's appeal was not wasted on Californians.

The election, which occurred on November 8, 1966, resulted in a landslide victory for the Republicans. Reagan walked away with 3,742,913 votes, which translated to the support of roughly 58 percent of state residents who cast a ballot. In comparison, Brown found favor with only 2,749,174 Californians, or 42 percent of the men and women who appeared at the polls that fall.

With his family at his side, Reagan was sworn in as governor on January 1, 1967. While he was excited about his new career and eager to attend to state affairs, he also grasped what huge difficulties lay ahead of him. Perhaps most significant, Reagan assumed leadership of a government that had been spending far more money than it was taking in. Though he had attracted voters with talk of lowering

Nancy and Reagan were photographed here immediately after he was elected governor. As he had predicted to her, they had set out on a political path that would forever change their lives.

taxes, it would not be easy to reduce any source of income to a state that already had a $194 million **budget deficit.**

Reagan later recalled preparing to take on the governorship—and all the challenges that accompanied it—armed with the knowledge that his job would not be simple. "I knew I had to do some quick homework . . . before arriving in Sacramento [California]," he noted. "After years of criticizing government, I was about to stick my head into the lions' den and the lions would be waiting for me."

FROM CALIFORNIA TO THE NATION'S CAPITAL Five

$\mathcal{D}$espite being faced with a massive budget deficit, Governor Reagan tried to avoid raising Californians' taxes. At first, he attempted to restore the state's finances by ordering all government agencies to cut their spending by 10 percent. He also issued a hiring freeze that restricted any new employees from being added to the staff, even if it was to replace a worker who quit or retired.

Unfortunately, Reagan—and the various government departments that would have been impacted by his proposed reductions—quickly discovered that his economic plan was impractical. Everything from state-financed social service agencies to public health organizations would not be able to run efficiently if they trimmed their funding to the new governor's specifications. Reagan therefore had little choice but to present a new budget to California **legislators**.

The final result was a bill that drastically raised Californians' taxes—hiking them to an extent that has yet to be matched by any other state increase in U.S. history. While the revised budget ran in complete contrast to what Reagan had initially envisioned for his governorship, it was not without its advantages. For starters, crafting it forced him to learn how to communicate openly and effectively with key members of the California Assembly, which is the state's legislative body. Even though the assembly was controlled by Democrats, Reagan still needed

As governor of California, Reagan was forced to tackle everything from economic issues like the budget deficit to moral controversies such as bills that had the power to legalize abortion.

to find a way to work with its members to balance the budget and address other important issues.

One such topic was an abortion bill that certain state legislators wanted him to sign in 1967. If made a law, the Therapeutic Abortion Act would allow women to legally terminate, or end, their pregnancies in certain circumstances. Politicians across the country who were members of both the Democratic and Republican parties were divided on the topic of abortion. Some considered it murder, while others regarded it as an expression of a woman's right to decide what to do with her own body.

Later in his political career, Reagan would become famous for his staunch views against abortion. In 1967, however, he was still in the process of educating himself about the medical procedure and all the moral, legal, and physical debates connected with it. In addition, he learned that many women in desperate situations were having illegal abortions performed in unsafe, unsanitary conditions because they did not have any alternative options. Reagan considered the health risks these individuals were compelled to take because they had nowhere else to turn. As a result, he signed the Therapeutic Abortion Act into law in June 1967. It allowed women who were victims of rape or incest to legally terminate their pregnancies. The legislation gave similar rights to patients whose health would be placed in jeopardy by carrying or delivering a baby.

Yet abortion was just one subject that Reagan had to tackle as governor. School riots and welfare **reforms** were topics he would eventually address while heading the state. In dealing with these issues, he did not always win praise. Some critics noted that he seemed to enjoy the ceremonial aspects of being governor but was remarkably hands-off when it came to actual politics.

They accused him of letting his aides and advisers play too great a role in influencing how the government was run. Reagan later emphasized how this could not have been farther from the truth.

"Some people have suggested . . . my cabinet meetings resembled the meetings of a corporation's board of directors," he remarked. "I suppose that's true, but there was one difference: We never took a vote. Everyone pitched in and was involved in the give and take of debate, but when the discussion was over, they all knew it was up to me and me alone to make the decision."

PLANNING FOR THE PRESIDENCY

Apparently, many average Californians knew this, too, and had enough admiration for Reagan's leadership to elect him to a second term of office in 1970. The race against Democratic candidate Jesse Unruh, who was the speaker of the California House of Representatives, was closer than it had been against Brown in 1966. Reagan won slightly less than 53 percent of the vote, while his chief opponent claimed about 45 percent.

By this time, however, the governor was already stretching his ambitions beyond the limits of statewide politics. As early as 1966 Reagan had thought about paving a career path that would ultimately lead to the White House. In 1967 he began discussing entering the Republican primaries that would precede the following year's presidential election. Reagan went on to formally declare his candidacy in the summer of 1968.

Though he was well known to both the Republican Party and members of the general public, he faced formidable opponents. Richard Nixon was the most notable of these and led a fierce campaign. The former vice president had several years of political experience behind him and had run against John Kennedy in an unsuccessful bid for the White House in 1960.

In comparison, Reagan had not yet served a full term as governor and put up nowhere near as hard a fight as his competitors for the nomination. For these reasons, as well as the fact that Nixon gained the support of influential politicians such as Barry Goldwater, Nixon was named the party's presidential candidate at the Republican National Convention in August 1968. Reagan later claimed that his failure to be selected as the nominee was—at that moment—a much-welcomed turn of events.

Nixon (shown here) claimed the presidential nomination at the Republican National Convention in August 1968. Though this meant Reagan had to wait for his chance at the White House, it gave him extra time to gain added political knowledge and experience.

"When Nixon was nominated, I was the most relieved person in the world," he emphasized. "I knew I wasn't ready to be president. I knew there was still . . . work to be done in Sacramento [California]." Part of this work involved passing the California Welfare Reform Act (CWRA) of 1971. Welfare is financial assistance that the government provides to people who are unable to support themselves, either because they are mentally or physically disabled or are dealing with long-term unemployment.

Despite the good it does for many citizens, this type of program places added strain on state funding. Reagan, who had been challenged by an enormous budget deficit from the time he entered office, was therefore eager to make sure that the people who were taking advantage of welfare truly needed it. The CWRA helped accomplish this goal by cracking down on individuals who committed fraud to receive government aid. It also increased restrictions on who was considered eligible for financial assistance. Just three years after the CWRA was enacted in 1971, California's welfare caseloads dropped by 17 percent, which saved taxpayers about $2 billion.

While this reform and other state affairs kept Reagan busy, he did not abandon his plans to ultimately seek out the Republican nomination for president a second time. His supporters hoped to get his name on the party's ticket as Nixon, who had won national elections in 1968 and 1972, neared the end of his second term in the White House. By 1974, though, a scandal emerged that promised to reshape the race Reagan had once imagined he would be running.

Working to Win the Nomination in 1976

Those Americans who had predicted they would watch Nixon bid farewell to crowds in Washington, D.C., in early 1977 probably never guessed that the nation's leader would say good-bye much sooner. When the president left the White House in August 1974, it was amidst a flurry of heated accusations. Nixon resigned more than two years before his term was to end as a result of his involvement in a scandal known as Watergate.

On June 17, 1972, a break-in occurred at the Watergate Hotel and office complex in Washington, D.C., where the Democratic National Committee was headquartered. The individuals responsible for the intrusion were eventually recognized as members of Nixon's Committee to Re-elect the President, who were looking to steal information. Nixon himself initially denied any connection to the wrongdoing. By 1974, however, it was becoming clear that Nixon was lying. In early June of that year, he was officially named a coconspirator in the Watergate break-in.

Before Congress could determine whether or not Nixon should be **impeached**, he resigned in disgrace—prompting Vice President Gerald Ford to assume leadership of the country. The previous December, Ford had become second in command to Nixon after

'I HAVE DISCOVERED THAT ACCORDING TO A SECRET TAPE OF JUNE 23, 1972, I **AM** A CROOK.'

This political cartoon from 1974 mocks Nixon's involvement in Watergate. His role in the scandal brought a crashing halt to his presidential career.

Vice President Spiro Agnew stepped down from office amidst charges of bribery. As the 1976 election neared, Ford declared that he was eager to spend another four years leading the country.

Reagan, however, refused to simply back away from the White House because of the change in circumstances that resulted from Watergate. He was far more determined to win the Republican nomination than he had been in 1968. Nor did he think that Ford was an effective leader or a strong enough candidate to guarantee the party control of the presidency. As a result, on November 20, 1975, Reagan announced his decision to run as a candidate in the Republican primaries.

Though Ford (shown here) was sworn into office after Nixon resigned in 1974, Reagan still challenged him for control of the White House during the 1976 Republican National Convention.

He had chosen not to pursue a third term as governor of California in 1974 and had spent the period that followed making political speeches, expressing his views on a nationally syndicated radio show, and writing a newspaper column. Reagan also continued to gain the support of conservative Republicans—several of whom regarded Ford's administration as too **liberal**. Adding to President Ford's unpopularity was the fact that he had granted Nixon a full pardon for his connection to Watergate in 1974. Many people felt Ford should have held Nixon accountable for his actions.

One of Ford's advantages over Reagan, however, was that he was an incumbent president. Candidates seeking a political position who hold office at the time they run in an election generally enjoy the backing of their party. Ford happily found this to be the case at the Republican National Convention that took place in the summer of 1976. He was declared the party's presidential candidate, but Reagan trailed behind by only 117 votes.

After a winning candidate is selected during the primaries, members of his or her party—even if they previously were competing for the same position—typically offer their support to the victor. Throughout the autumn of 1976, however, Ford discovered that he could expect little help from his former Republican opponent along the campaign trail against Democratic nominee James "Jimmy" Carter Junior. Reagan grudgingly spoke in favor of Ford but often claimed that prior commitments prevented him from more actively campaigning for him. In reality, Reagan was already busy thinking about the presidential election of 1980.

After the polls closed on Election Day in 1976, the Democrats celebrated a triumph over Ford. Reagan realized that, if he

Reagan and Nancy were at hand when Ford won the nomination at the 1976 Republican National Convention. Yet, as the public would learn in the years that followed, Reagan had no intention of abandoning his own ambitions for the presidency.

received the Republican nomination in the next race for the White House, he would be running against Carter. For his part, Reagan was looking toward the future.

"After Ford's loss," he observed, "I knew some of my supporters would begin knocking on my door and urge me to run in 1980, and they did. . . . I wanted to be president. But I really believed that what happened next wasn't up to me, it was up to the people. If there was a real people's movement to get me to run, then I said I'd do it." As the four years ahead would reveal, Reagan would not disappoint his supporters.

Ford's Views on Reagan

Throughout his career, Ford expressed multiple opinions of Reagan. On the one hand, he noted in 2004 that the fortieth president was "an excellent leader of our nation during challenging times at home and abroad." When Ford passed away in 2006, however, newspaper interviews surfaced that reflected a far more critical attitude.

Based on these accounts, Ford took a harsh view of Reagan's leadership abilities, declaring that he was "probably the least well-informed on the details of running the government of any president I knew." Ford also remarked that his former competitor for the 1976 Republican nomination "was just a poor manager, and you can't be president and do a good job unless you manage."

Winning and Working in the White House

*F*ortunately for Reagan, Jimmy Carter's presidency was filled with situations that put the president at a disadvantage by the time 1980 approached. For starters the 1970s were an era of higher unemployment than the previous decade. To make matters worse, the economy had been crippled by soaring inflation rates. Inflation occurs when there is a general and progressive rise in the prices of goods and services. Combined with the widespread unemployment throughout the United States, steep inflation rates led to stagflation, or a period when the economy shows few signs of growth.

Adding to Carter's troubles were international relations with the Middle Eastern country of Iran. In November 1979 Iranian students took fifty-two Americans hostage. The kidnappers were devoted followers of the **Ayatollah** Khomeini, who had recently assumed power after the **shah** abandoned control of the nation.

Tensions between the new Islamic leader and the Carter administration increased when the shah was allowed to reside temporarily in the United States. Radicals loyal to the ayatollah protested by storming the U.S. embassy in Iran. When several American citizens there were taken hostage, their families and friends looked to Carter to secure their freedom. Yet, even as the upcoming national election loomed, the president was unable to

As of November 1980, anti-American feelings were evident outside the U.S. Embassy in Iran. Protestors expressed their low opinions of Carter by hanging a cardboard likeness of him from a scaffold.

arrange for their release. Negotiations stalled, and an attempted rescue by the military failed.

Though Reagan was careful not to use the sensitive hostage situation as a campaign tool, that crisis—along with the sluggish economy—undeniably worked in his favor. In the summer of 1980 he was named the Republican presidential nominee.

With former Texas congressman George H. W. Bush as his vice-presidential running mate, he proceeded to wage an aggressive and successful battle against Carter.

Nevertheless, Reagan's victory was by no means assured. Carter was quick to point out that his opponent was extremely conservative and far more right wing than Nixon or Ford had been. He also criticized Reagan's resistance to forging agreements with the Soviet Union to restrict the number of arms each nation built up throughout the cold war. Carter's supporters relied on such issues to portray the Republican nominee as a **warmonger**, and an aging one at that.

Reagan was already sixty-nine, which—if he triumphed over the Democrats—would make him the oldest elected president in U.S. history. Despite his advanced years, his political experience was still limited to the governorship of California. As Americans prepared to cast their ballots in November 1980, they considered these factors. On the other hand, they reflected on how Carter was leading a country that was in the middle of a hostage crisis and that was shaken by an unstable economy. Shortly before Election Day, Reagan gave voters a final point to keep in mind as they headed to the polls.

"It might be well if you would ask yourself, 'Are you better off than you were four years ago?'" he remarked during a televised debate with Carter on October 28, 1980. "Is it easier for you to go and buy things in the stores than it was four years ago? Is there more or less unemployment in the country than there was four years ago? Is America as respected throughout the world as it was? Do you feel that our security is as safe, that we're as strong as we were four years ago? And if you answer all

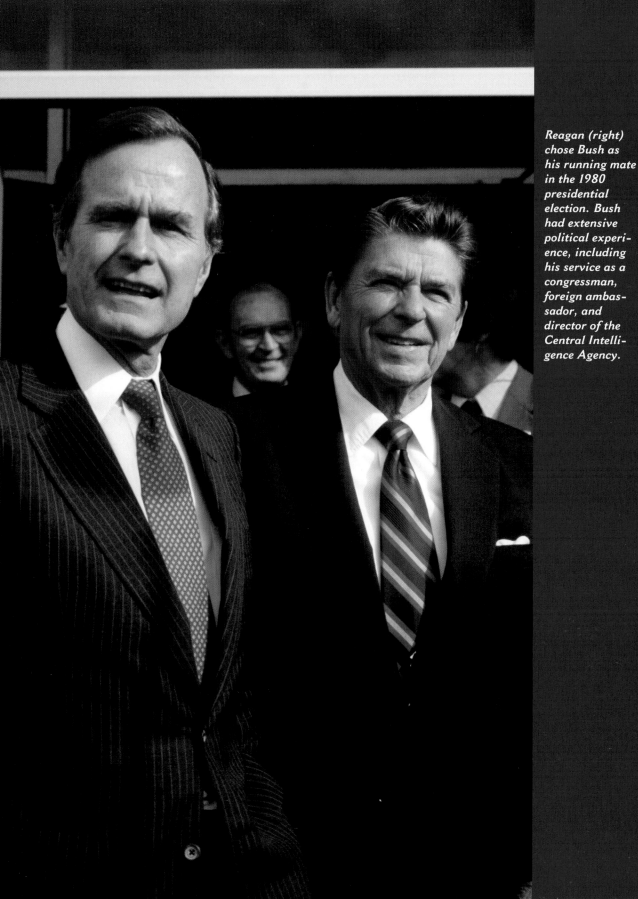

Reagan (right) chose Bush as his running mate in the 1980 presidential election. Bush had extensive political experience, including his service as a congressman, foreign ambassador, and director of the Central Intelligence Agency.

of those questions yes, why then, I think your choice is very obvious as to whom you will vote for. If you don't agree, if you don't think that this course that we've been on for the last four years is what you would like to see us follow for the next four, then I could suggest another choice that you have." In the end U.S. citizens responded with a firm no to most of the questions he asked—and with a resounding yes to the idea of Reagan as their fortieth president.

THE REALITIES OF REAGANOMICS

On November 4, 1980, Americans cast 43,903,230 ballots in Reagan's favor. Carter won just 35,480,115 votes by comparison. Results in the Electoral College reflected a much more decisive victory for the Republicans. A total of 489 electors backed Reagan, versus 49 who supported Carter.

On January 20, 1981, the Hollywood actor-turned-politician was sworn into the nation's highest office. The same day he assumed the responsibilities of leading the country, Iranian kidnappers freed the American hostages whom they had held for more than a year. Though Carter had been negotiating their release for months, much of the glory surrounding their liberation went to Reagan.

The new president, however, had little time to celebrate the event. Just as he had been confronted with a massive budget deficit when he became governor of California, so did he find himself challenged by nationwide economic crises in 1981. In 1980 the rate of inflation had climbed to double digits and had reached about 13.5 percent. This figure represents the amount that average prices for goods and services increase over the course of a year. To put that percentage in perspective, the annual rate of

When Reagan took the oath of office in January 1981, he assumed responsibility for a nation in the midst of several economic and diplomatic crises.

inflation in the United States has not risen beyond 10 percent since 1982. Most years it has remained below 5 percent.

In addition to the problem of inflation, Reagan was acting as head of state within a nation where, in 1981, 7.6 percent of the workforce was unemployed. In an effort to improve America's economic situation, he pushed Congress to adopt financial policies that experts eventually began to refer to as "Reaganomics." His plan to help U.S. citizens recover from the troubles they had begun to experience during the Carter administration involved decreasing government spending in certain areas and reducing its regulation of businesses.

Unlike many attempts by previous presidents to balance the budget, Reagan's plan relied heavily on the idea of cutting taxes. In the late summer of 1981 Reagan signed the Economic Recovery Tax Act (ERTA) into law. This legislation provided for a 25-percent decrease in taxes over a period of three years. Along with members of Congress who supported the ERTA, Reagan hoped it would stimulate long-term growth by allowing people to save money and to invest more money in the stock market. In turn, he believed that employment rates would increase. Reagan was optimistic that, over time, U.S. citizens would earn more taxable income. This would mean more government revenue, which would help balance the national budget.

When Reagan concluded his second term in office in 1988, the economy had ultimately improved. That year, only 5.5 percent of the workforce reported being unemployed, and the rate of inflation had fallen to 4.1 percent. Economic recovery was not immediate, though. In fact, things actually got worse before they got better, and Reaganomics was at the center of various debates and controversies.

When his proposed tax cuts were set in motion, critics argued that they were of far greater benefit to wealthy citizens who were earning sizable salaries than to poor or middle-class families. In response, politicians who were in favor of Reaganomics emphasized that the president's policies would still help men and women from these last two groups. They reasoned that business owners and company heads who owed fewer taxes would in turn be able to invest more money in the stock market, hire additional workers, and pay higher wages.

Unfortunately, as of 1982, many Americans were finding it difficult to appreciate how Reagan's plan had done much to improve their lives. By that point the nation had fallen into a recession, or an extended period of economic decline, leaving one in ten U.S. workers without a job. The government also struggled with record budget deficits. Reagan's critics complained that the country's financial situation had not seemed so bleak since the Great Depression, decades before. Some also observed that he had slashed government funding to programs that were designed to aid the poor but had boosted military spending.

In 1983, however, things started to look up. Despite the damage it had caused, the recession managed to drive down prices on goods and services, since people had less money to spend on them. The result was that the rate of inflation dropped, and the stock market grew. Though it took time, the American economy began to recover and, as it did, the president simultaneously dealt with a variety of issues related to international affairs.

ADDRESSING INTERNATIONAL UNREST

Throughout his first term in office, Reagan and Congress had struggled to analyze the budget and determine where cuts could be made. One portion of government spending that the president refused to slash was military defense. He even proposed an increase in defense funding over a period of five years that amounted to a budget of $15 trillion.

From Reagan's perspective the country's military forces needed to be strengthened so that America could hold its own as a world power whose citizens took a firm stand against threats such as communism. During the 1980s the United States remained involved in the cold war with the Soviet Union, which supported

Surviving an Assassination Attempt

Shortly after he took office, Reagan came close to losing his life to an assassin's bullet. On March 30, 1981, a mentally unstable man named John Hinckley Junior shot the president as he left a hotel in Washington, D.C. Three other people were injured by gunfire during the assassination attempt.

Secret Service agents rushed Reagan to a local hospital, where he was treated for a pierced lung. Fortunately, he recovered quickly and was applauded by his colleagues when he appeared before Congress less than a month later. Hinckley was later found to be insane and was committed to a psychiatric institution. He reportedly hoped that his plot to murder Reagan would impress the actress Jodie Foster, with whom he was obsessed at the time.

Reagan was eager that Americans increase their military preparedness and encouraged government spending that boosted construction of weapons and equipment such as the fighter plane shown here.

other communist nations in Asia, Africa, and Latin America. Reagan was determined to oppose oppressive governments who he feared were intent on destroying democracy.

"I believe that communism is another sad, bizarre chapter in human history whose last pages even now are being written," he declared during a speech in March 1983. That same month Reagan proposed the Strategic Defense Initiative (SDI). The idea behind the SDI was to use both ground and satellite devices to seek out and destroy enemy missiles before they reached U.S. targets.

Though the Reagan administration poured billions of dollars into researching this technological shield, it never became a reality. Critics who doubted the effectiveness of the defense program mockingly called it "Star Wars" in reference to the popular science-fiction movies that were released in the late 1970s and early 1980s. Yet, while the SDI did not materialize, some people think it helped end the cold war because it cast doubt on the Soviets' ability to successfully attack America.

It would be several more years, however, before tensions between both nations officially resolved. In the meantime, Reagan was confronted with crises that extended beyond Eastern Europe. For example, violence claimed the lives of 241 U.S. servicemen in Beirut, Lebanon, on October 23, 1983.

Bloody conflicts in that Middle Eastern country frequently pitted Muslims against Christians. Fighting also erupted when Muslims in Lebanon who were part of a political movement known as the Palestinian Liberation Organization (PLO) clashed with Israeli forces to the south. The United States and various European nations dispatched peacekeeping troops to the Lebanese capital of Beirut during the early 1980s in the hopes of calming growing violence there.

Unsurprisingly, not everyone in the Middle East welcomed a foreign military presence. This was made painfully clear on October 23, 1983, when two trucks loaded with explosives were driven into military barracks in Beirut, killing a total of 299 servicemen. Of that number, 241 were Americans. U.S. intelligence suggested that a Muslim terrorist group known as Hezbollah was responsible for the attacks and may have been aided by the Iranian government.

Attacks on the marine barracks in Beirut shocked the world and forced Reagan to rethink his strategies in Lebanon.

Reagan initially vowed to retaliate, or seek revenge, and announced that he would not remove American peacekeeping forces from Lebanon. By February 1984, however, his concern for the safety of U.S. troops there prompted him to order their withdrawal. It would not be the last time the United States clashed with Hezbollah during Reagan's presidency.

Nor could he focus exclusively on problems in the Middle East. Trouble brewing in the Caribbean nation of Grenada made news headlines in 1983 as well. That year, communist revolutionaries took control of the island.

U.S. intervention in Grenada helped stamp out Communism in the Caribbean, though America and communist nations like the Soviet Union were still a long way from ending the cold war.

Reagan worried that the shift in government would allow the Soviet Union to use Grenada as an airbase in the Americas. He was also concerned that the Soviets would be able to increase their communist influence in nearby countries. Finally, Reagan feared for the safety of nearly six hundred American students who were attending a Grenadian medical school.

Reagan ordered U.S. forces to invade Grenada on October 25, 1983, with the purpose of overthrowing its communist government. The military operation, which was a success, lasted less than a week and ended with American troops returning home by the following December. Despite recent events in Lebanon, Reagan was therefore able to approach the upcoming election with an undeniable victory over communism. Both his opponents and supporters wondered, though, if his accomplishments from 1981 to 1984 would be enough to keep him in the White House for a second term.

THE ROUGH ROAD TO A BETTER TOMORROW *Seven*

*I*n late 1984 reelection was not necessarily guaranteed for seventy-three-year-old President Reagan, who was running against Democratic nominee Walter Mondale. On the one hand the U.S. economy was showing new signs of life, and America continued to take a tough—and sometimes successful—stand against communism. On the other, the nation had experienced a recession under his leadership, and his critics argued that the famous tax cuts of Reaganomics had benefited the wealthy far more than they had the lower and middle classes.

THE ISSUE OF AGE

During his 1984 campaign, Mondale did not shy away from reminding voters that Reagan was the oldest head of state in U.S. history. For his part the president used his famous sense of humor to shrug off suggestions that he was too advanced in years to perform the duties of office. He emphasized that he was at the peak of physical fitness and hinted that perhaps Mondale's bigger concern should be that he was only fifty-six. "I will not make age an issue in this campaign," Reagan joked during one televised debate. "I'm not going to exploit for political purposes my opponent's youth and inexperience."

Neither Mondale nor his supporters could deny that the Great Communicator was extremely popular with many Americans. Some citizens did worry that he took too much of a hands-off approach to government by allowing his advisers—and even Nancy—more influence than they possibly should have had on day-to-day politics. Luckily for Reagan, though, such concerns did not cost him the 1984 election.

On November 6 of that year roughly 59 percent of American voters threw their support behind the president. Approximately 54,455,472 ballots were cast in his favor on Election Day, and he claimed the backing of 525 members of the Electoral College. In contrast, Mondale walked away from the race with 37,577,352 votes and the favor of just 13 electors. Reagan reflected on both the past and the future as he prepared to serve the country for another term in office.

"When I took this oath four years ago, I did so in a time of economic stress," he declared during his inaugural address on January 21, 1985. "Voices were raised saying that we had to look to our past for the greatness and glory. But we, the present-day Americans, are not given to looking backward. In this blessed land, there is always a better tomorrow."

For Reagan it was crucial to see the future he spoke of shaped by the United States' ongoing fight against communism. In early 1985 shifts in the Soviet administration seemed to hint at promising changes in the course the cold war was taking. At about that time an ambitious and energetic politician named Mikhail Gorbachev had risen to the position of General Secretary of the Communist Party of the Soviet Union. Some Americans did not initially feel that he would prove better or worse than the leaders who had come before him. Yet it would

Gorbachev (seated, left) and Reagan eventually shaped a political friendship that helped ease many of the tensions between the United States and the Soviet Union.

be Gorbachev's work with Reagan that ultimately concluded the forty-six-year cold war.

This outcome, however, was still years away, and in 1985 the U.S. president was not able to concentrate all his efforts on addressing relations with the Soviet Union. Reagan also used his second term to strengthen what was referred to as the nation's War on Drugs, since illegal narcotics were becoming a growing problem on America's streets. In 1986 he signed a bill that provided the government with almost $2 billion to help combat drug trafficking and abuse. Part of this legislation set mandatory minimum punishments for people who committed drug-related offenses.

Cracking down on illegal drugs played a role in Reagan's plan to create the "better tomorrow" he mentioned at his second inauguration ceremony. Unfortunately, America's future in the years following his reelection was not always a happy one. And on January 28, 1986, Reagan was faced with the task of helping a grieving nation heal.

Coping with Tragedy and Terrorism

On that date men, women, and children across the country excitedly tuned into their television sets. They were eager to watch the space shuttle *Challenger* take off from the Kennedy Space Center in Cape Canaveral, Florida. Within minutes, however, their anticipation was replaced by horror as they witnessed the spacecraft explode.

All seven crew members, including a New Hampshire high school teacher named Christa McAuliffe, died. She had been aboard as part of the National Aeronautics and Space Administration (NASA)-sponsored Teacher in Space Project, which was developed to inspire knowledge about space travel in U.S. schools. It was later determined that mechanical problems had led to the explosion, but that did little to ease the shock and pain that crippled the nation following the disaster. In response to the events of January 28, 1986, Reagan tried to console and reassure Americans via a televised address.

"There will be more shuttle flights and more shuttle crews and, yes, more volunteers, more civilians, more teachers in space," he promised. "Nothing ends here; our hopes and our journeys continue." The final part of this message was particularly important for U.S. citizens to hear, especially since they had already been confronted with several other crises during Reagan's second term.

The Challenger *was only seventy-two seconds into its flight when it exploded.*

Starting in the summer of 1985, Middle Eastern Muslim terrorist groups had organized a series of hijackings in their continued struggles with Israel and its allies. On June 14, 1985, Lebanese **extremists** took control of TWA Flight 847, which was transporting 153 passengers—about half of whom were Americans. The hijackers forced the plane to land in Beirut, Lebanon, and killed one U.S. serviceman who was aboard.

As the weeks passed, the extremists refused to free all of their hostages unless certain demands were met. These included the liberation of hundreds of Muslim prisoners from Israeli jails. Despite the fact that several Americans were involved in the hijacking, Reagan vowed that he would not negotiate with terrorists or with any foreign government on behalf of their interests. Eventually, the Israelis started to release their Muslim captives. Yet Reagan continued to emphasize that his administration had not brokered a deal between that nation and the extremists connected to TWA Flight 847. Thankfully, the remaining hostages were freed by the beginning of July 1985.

Not even a year had passed, however, before Reagan was compelled to deal with new international tensions. This time it came in the form of conflict with Libya. Since 1969 that African country had been run by a former military leader named Mu'ammar Al-Gadhafi, who was known to have forged relationships with terrorist organizations that posed a threat to U.S. interests.

Al-Gadhafi (shown here) continues to remain in control of Libya today.

Libyans walk amidst the wreckage of one of their villages following U.S. military strikes in April 1986.

In March 1986 American troops and Al-Gadhafi's forces clashed in the Gulf of Sidra, which is located in the Mediterranean Sea off the northern coast of Libya. U.S. military officials insisted that they had a right to be there, noting that their ships were more than 12 miles from the shoreline. This is the nautical measurement most nations use to mark territorial boundaries. Nevertheless, Al-Gadhafi ordered an attack on American vessels that had sailed into the gulf. The United States answered Libyan hostilities by firing back on their ships and radar systems. The following month Al-Gadhafi retaliated by encouraging a terrorist plot that resulted in the bombing of a disco in West Germany. Two people were killed, including one U.S. serviceman, and two hundred others were injured. On April 14, 1986, Reagan responded by authorizing a massive military strike against Libya.

The main objective of the assault was to reduce Al-Gadhafi's ability to aid international terrorism. American missiles hit training bases, weapons depots, barracks, defense systems, and airfields.

After the strike had already been under way for a few hours, Reagan delivered a televised speech to the nation.

"When our citizens are attacked or abused anywhere in the world on the direct orders of hostile regimes, we will respond so long as I'm in this office," the president proclaimed. Yet not everyone admired Reagan's protective attitude. In fact, nations such as Iran, China, and the Soviet Union condemned the U.S. assault and pointed out that it had cost fifteen Libyan civilians their lives. If Reagan's role in the military strike stirred debate, however, it hardly compared to the controversy that swirled around his diplomatic relations in the months ahead.

TRADING ARMS FOR AMERICAN LIVES

During the mid–1980s the United States was caught in the middle of several international tensions that ranged from being merely uncomfortable to openly explosive. The first half of Reagan's presidency had been impacted by hostilities that stretched from the Caribbean to the Middle East. In the final four years of his administration, America would play a part in conflicts that spanned an equally broad portion of the globe. But it was the nation's diplomatic relations with Nicaragua and Iran that would be at the center of a major scandal that occurred during Reagan's second term in office.

Starting in the late 1970s, terrorist groups such as Hezbollah had begun making news headlines by taking U.S. and European hostages. The kidnappings were frequently used to protest Western military involvement in warfare between Christian and Muslim groups throughout the Middle East. From 1982 to 1992 terrorists had captured ninety-six foreign hostages in Lebanon.

Although its leaders never publicly assumed responsibility for the kidnappings, Hezbollah was believed to be behind them, as were the governments of Iran and Syria. Several experts suspected that Middle Eastern terrorists held some of the hostages as a means of guarding against U.S. retaliation for their 1984 attacks on American army barracks in Lebanon. Others think they hoped to force the United States to provide military and economic aid to countries like Iran, which had been at war with the neighboring nation of Iraq since 1980.

Regardless of the kidnappers' motivations, the lives of their hostages were at risk, and Reagan's policy of refusing to negotiate with terrorists was called into question. As the years passed, the victims' families and friends—as well as the American public in general—grew more impatient for their release. Then, in 1985, Israeli officials contacted members of Reagan's administration and informed them that supposedly moderate Iranians could help convince Hezbollah to free the hostages.

The individuals who indicated they were willing to aid U.S. victims allegedly opposed the Ayatollah Khomeini, with whom the United States had experienced tense relations for some time. These Iranians implied to Israel that they were interested in forming a friendship with America and said they could see to it that the hostages were liberated as part of a military weapons deal. Yet, while the offer had its appeal, it also presented a complicated situation for Reagan.

For starters, he had famously sworn off bargaining with nations who harbored terrorists, including Iran. Selling weapons to such a country represented an illegal transaction. On the other hand, if it was conducted quietly, Reagan reasoned it could result in the safe return of U.S. hostages. Ultimately, he agreed to the deal—though it was a decision he would come to regret.

Involvement in the Iran-Contra Affair

As 1985 drew to a close, the original plan to use Israel as a middleman in the sale of weapons to Iran in exchange for the release of American hostages was altered. In December of that year an aide to the U.S. National Security Council named Oliver North proposed selling the arms directly to Iranian buyers. He also suggested that some of the profits be used to fund the efforts of **guerilla** fighters in the Central American republic of Nicaragua.

The Contras, as these forces were called, were waging attacks intended to overthrow the country's radical government. Reagan supported the Nicaraguan guerillas, but a collection of laws known as the Boland Amendments prohibited him from granting them weapons or aiding their rebellion. Yet members of his administration, including North and National Security Adviser John Poindexter, saw the Iranian arms deal as a way to secretly work around this legislation.

In November 1986, however, news of what became referred to as the Iran-Contra Affair leaked to the media. Reagan, who realized that his name had been linked to various foreign policy violations, claimed he had not been aware of all the details of the arrangement. He even appointed a special government review board called the Tower Commission to investigate the matter. Members of this panel interviewed more than eighty witnesses, including Reagan. Though the president admitted some knowledge of transactions involving the Iran-Contra Affair, he implied that his aides were primarily responsible for any illegal dealings that may have taken place. It was eventually determined that between $10 million and $30 million from weapons sales to Iran had been channeled to the guerilla movement in Nicaragua. By February 1987 the Tower Commission concluded that, though Reagan was not guilty of a crime, his mismanagement had enabled government aides to break the law.

Fourteen members of his administration faced criminal charges related to the scandal; eleven were convicted. North and Poindexter were among this latter group, but rulings against them were overturned on technicalities. In the years to come several of the other individuals who had been found guilty were pardoned. Though Middle Eastern terrorists did release a few of the

All charges against North (shown here) in the Iran-Contra Affair were finally dismissed in September 1991.

Western hostages after 1986, some experts believe that a handful of new American victims were kidnapped a short while later to take their place.

Following the Iran-Contra Affair, Reagan's popularity rating plummeted. In the weeks before the scandal broke, 67 percent of U.S. citizens approved of his job performance. Only 40 percent expressed the same opinion in March 1987. In many people's minds, if Reagan was not guilty of dealing with terrorists and violating the Boland Amendments outright, he at least had to admit that he poorly supervised his staff.

"I take full responsibility for my own actions and for those of my administration," he declared during a televised speech in early 1987. "As disappointed as I may be in some who served me, I'm still the one who must answer to the American people for this behavior." Luckily for Reagan, the Iran-Contra Affair would not be the only foreign diplomacy for which he is remembered.

Final Years of the Fortieth President

*R*eagan's image was undoubtedly tarnished by the Iran-Contra Affair. Yet many U.S. citizens felt that whatever mistakes he made in this situation were balanced by his successes in helping to conclude the cold war. Reagan openly expressed his hope that the Soviet Union would collapse, effectively ending that nation's communist influence over other parts of the world.

Until that day arrived, however, he recognized the importance of easing cold war tensions. Eventually, he and his administration began to perceive in Mikhail Gorbachev a foreign leader who might be able to make this happen. Reagan and the General Secretary of the Communist Party of the Soviet Union discussed issues of diplomacy at five official meetings that took place between 1985 and 1988. Gorbachev knew that his nation's continued arms race with the United States was costing a great deal of money that the government could not afford to keep spending.

By the early 1980s it appeared that the Soviets had built up a military presence and weapons collection that rivaled those of America. During his first term Reagan pushed to increase America's defense budget. As the decade wore on, the Soviets became unable to keep up. The money they had already pumped into efforts to get ahead in the arms race had put a strain on the Soviet economy. Soviet finances were also weakened by communist principles that included government-controlled manufacturing and the common ownership of farms.

When Gorbachev first rose to power, he planned to make changes in his administration and in international policy that would revitalize communism. First he began removing politicians from power who still dreamed of Soviet world domination and the destruction of the United States. He also reformed numerous domestic policies so that ordinary citizens could earn more money and enjoy a higher standard of living. Finally, Gorbachev gave people greater personal liberties, such as freedom of speech and freedom to travel. They had not enjoyed many of these rights under former Soviet leaders.

Reagan obviously did not share Gorbachev's ambition to breathe new life into communism. He therefore supported reforms suggested by the Soviet official that granted people an increased voice in government and that ended several of the oppressive practices associated with communist rule.

Just as important, both officials worked to reduce their arms buildup. In 1987 they even agreed to destroy thousands of nuclear missiles and to submit to inspections of each other's military bases. As relations between the two nations continued to improve and Gorbachev pushed for additional Soviet reforms, a series of historic changes were set into motion. By 1991 the cold war had concluded, communism had collapsed in Eastern Europe, and the Soviet Union had fallen.

In 1992 the current Russian Federation was created. It is made up of eighty-three individual territories and regions that are all unified under a central government shaped by the principles of democracy. These developments followed a decade

"Tear Down This Wall!"

On June 12, 1987, Reagan publicly called on Gorbachev to help eliminate the oppressive influence that communism had outside the Soviet Union. On that day the American president stood alongside the  Berlin Wall, which separated East Germany from West Germany. The massive cement barrier symbolized the division that split what had formerly been the country of Germany following World War II.

The East had a communist government, while the West supported democracy. In the years since the war West Germans had built a powerful, thriving nation. East Germans, on the other hand, struggled to survive and prosper amidst the economic and political restrictions set in place by communism.

In the summer of 1987 Reagan reminded the public of these differences as he gave a speech to an enthusiastic crowd gathered beneath the wall. "General Secretary Gorbachev," he challenged, "if you seek peace, if you seek prosperity for the Soviet Union and Eastern Europe, if you seek liberalization, come here to this gate. Mr. Gorbachev, open this gate. Mr. Gorbachev, tear down this wall!" The Berlin Wall ultimately did fall in November 1989 and signaled the overall collapse of communism in Eastern Europe.

during which Reagan and Gorbachev proved to people across the globe that it was possible for former enemies to work together to promote peace and reform. Besides improving diplomatic relations between two world powers, both men gradually came to respect one another.

"A true leader, a man of his word and an optimist, he . . . has earned a place in history and in people's hearts," Gorbachev ultimately declared of Reagan. As the second term of America's fortieth president drew to a close, many of his supporters shared similar sentiments. Yet whether people adored Reagan for what he had accomplished or criticized him for his faults, it was time for him to leave the White House in 1989.

The Sunset of a Leader's Life

In November 1988 Vice President George H. W. Bush beat Democratic candidate Michael Dukakis during that year's presidential election. After watching his successor sworn into office, Reagan departed Washington, D.C., with Nancy at his side on January 20, 1989, and headed back to California. Earlier that month he had delivered his televised farewell address to the nation:

> I won a nickname, "The Great Communicator." But I never thought it was my style or the words I used that made a difference: It was the content. I wasn't a great communicator, but I communicated great things, and they didn't spring full bloom from my brow, they came from the heart of a great nation—from our experience, our wisdom, and our belief in the principles that have guided us for two centuries. They called it the Reagan revolution. Well, I'll accept that, but for me it always seemed more like the great rediscovery, a rediscovery of our values and our common sense.

Following eight years of rediscovery Ronald and Nancy Reagan moved their belongings out of the White House. They then settled into a home in Los Angeles, California, and at a ranch about 90 miles away, in Santa Barbara. Though Reagan was no longer leader of the nation, he continued to give speeches in support of various Republican politicians and charitable causes that he considered important. Reagan also wrote a best-selling autobiography titled *An American Life* that was published in 1990.

The Reagans frequently enjoyed horseback riding on their ranch in Santa Barbara in the years following his presidency.

Reagan (second from left) stands alongside (from left to right) Bush, Carter, Ford, and Nixon at the opening of the Ronald W. Reagan Presidential Library and Museum.

The next year he watched the Ronald W. Reagan Presidential Library and Museum in Simi Valley, California, open its doors for the first time. The three presidents who had preceded him—Richard Nixon, Gerald Ford, and Jimmy Carter—attended his library's opening ceremony on November 4, 1991. George H.W. Bush, who was already halfway through his only term in office, was present as well. The library currently houses approximately 50 million documents, 1.6 million photographs, and 40,000 artifacts linked to Reagan's administration.

Sadly, life for Reagan following his stay in the White House was not shaped by just speeches and events that honored his contributions to the United States. On November 5, 1994, he revealed to the public that he was suffering from Alzheimer's disease. This condition, which affects a person's central nervous system and causes brain cells to die off, typically results in severe confusion and memory loss. At the time Reagan announced his health status in 1994, there were no effective treatments or cures for Alzheimer's.

As Reagan grew older, it became increasingly harder for him to make public appearances due to his advancing Alzheimer's.

"I now begin the journey that will lead me into the sunset of my life," he shared in a letter to U.S. citizens. "I know that for America there will always be a bright dawn ahead." For Reagan, however, the next nine and a half years were sometimes dark and difficult.

He tried to remain active by walking, hiking, and educating himself about current political affairs. As with so many Alzheimer's patients, though, Reagan's mental state declined until he no longer even recognized members of his family. Not wanting Americans to see their former leader in this condition, Nancy increasingly limited his public appearances.

On June 5, 2004, he died in his home in Los Angeles due to pneumonia and other complications related to Alzheimer's. A state funeral was held six days later at Washington National Cathedral in the nation's capital. Reagan's friends, relatives, and political colleagues were among the 104,684 individuals who passed by his coffin to pay their respects. When funeral services concluded, his body was flown back to California, where it was buried on the grounds of the presidential library and museum in Simi Valley.

How Reagan Is Remembered

To this day, people all over the world have different opinions on Reagan's years in the White House and his legacy as a leader. From the perspective of his supporters, he played an important role in strengthening conservative ideas and rebuilding the U.S. economy after Carter's administration. Many also credit him with ending the cold war and helping stamp out oppressive communist governments across the globe.

On the other hand, Reagan's critics do not always agree with how he handled diplomatic situations involving terrorism. They often point out his questionable role in the Iran-Contra Affair. In addition, some people insist that his conservative views benefited wealthier citizens but led to harsher treatment of the nation's poor and middle classes.

More than three decades after Reagan was elected president, some Americans remember him as the Great Communicator. Others look upon him as a warmonger or a politician who was too hands-off in government affairs—unless they involved issues that interested him personally. Yet what no one can deny is that Reagan faced multiple challenges during his time in office and had unique approaches to improving and protecting the United States. The following quotation, which is carved into the walls surrounding his gravesite, sums up the ideas and values that defined his presidency:

"I know in my heart that man is good," the inscription reads. "That what is right will always eventually triumph, and that there is purpose and worth to each and every life." For Reagan, his purpose was to serve America and to fight for changes and ideals that he believed were in its people's best interests.

Americans and people all over the world may remember Reagan differently, but there is little debate that he had both an exciting and challenging presidency that forever shaped U.S. history.

TIMELINE

1911
Born in Tampico, Illinois, on
February 6

1940
Marries actress Jane Wyman

1949
Divorces Wyman

1952
Marries actress Nancy Davis

1966
Elected governor of
California

1968
Reelected to a second term
as governor of California

1970
Loses the presidential
nomination to Richard
Nixon

1910

1976
Campaigns to win the Republican nomination for president but loses to incumbent president Gerald Ford

1980
Beats Jimmy Carter in a national election to become the fortieth president of the United States

1984
Beats Democratic challenger Walter Mondale to win a second term in office

1989
Leaves the White House and returns to California

1994
Reveals he is suffering from Alzheimer's disease

2004
Dies in his home in Los Angeles, California

2010

NOTES

CHAPTER ONE

p. 7, "To sit back, hoping . . .": Ronald Reagan, quoted in the Federal Bureau of Investigation, "Remarks by Robert S. Mueller, III, Director, Federal Bureau of Investigation, InfraGard 2005 National Conference, Washington, D.C., August 9, 2005," *The Federal Bureau of Investigation Major Executive Speeches*, August 9, 2005, www.fbi.gov/pressrel/speeches/mueller080905.htm (accessed December 27, 2009).

p. 10, "a fat Dutchman": Jack Reagan, quoted in Lee Edwards, *The Essential Ronald Reagan: A Profile in Courage, Justice, and Wisdom* (Lanham, MD: Rowman & Littlefield, 2004), 5.

p. 10, "I learned from my . . .": Ronald Reagan, *An American Life* (New York: Simon & Schuster, 1990), 22.

p. 12, "Life is just one . . . .": Ronald Reagan, quoted in Jon C. Hopwood, "Ronald Reagan: The Most Successful Actor in World History," *Associated Content*, October 15, 2007, www.associatedcontent.com/article/415589/ronald_reagan_the_most_successful_actor.html (accessed January 21, 2010).

p. 12, "photographic mind": Quoted in Lou Cannon, *Ronald Reagan: The Presidential Portfolio: A History Illustrated from the Collection of the Ronald Reagan Library and Museum* (New York: PublicAffairs, 2001), 8.

p. 14, "Giving that speech . . . ": Ronald Reagan, quoted in Robert V. Friedenberg, *Notable Speeches in Contemporary Presidential Campaigns* (Westport, CT: Praeger, 2002), 146.

CHAPTER TWO

p. 16, "How do you get . . .": Ronald Reagan, quoted in Roger Rosenblatt, "1980: Ronald Reagan," *TIME*, January 2, 1981, www.time.com/time/subscriber/personoftheyear/archive/stories/1980.html (accessed December 26, 2009).

p. 17, "As staff announcer, I . . .": Reagan, *An American Life*, 70.

p. 19, "another Robert Taylor": Lou Cannon, *Governor Reagan: His Rise to Power* (New York: Public Affairs, 2003), 97.

p. 19, "I'd accomplished my goal . . .": Reagan, *An American Life*, 71.

p. 21, "On a Monday morning . . .": Reagan, *An American Life*, 84.

p. 22, "Some day when things are . . .": Quoted in Cannon, *Ronald Reagan: The Presidential Portfolio*, 15.

CHAPTER THREE

p. 29, "As I look back now . . .": Reagan, *An American Life*, 102–103.

p. 34, "He often seems remote . . .": Nancy Reagan, quoted in Cannon, *Governor Reagan*, 80.

p. 35, "I think everybody expected . . .": Reagan, *An American Life*, 127.

p. 35, "Those GE tours became . . .": Reagan, *An American Life*, 129.

CHAPTER FOUR

p. 41, "You and I have . . .": Ronald Reagan, quoted in Gleaves Whitney, "Ronald Reagan, R.I.P.," *The National Review*, January 7, 2004, www.nationalreview.com/comment/whitney200406070843.asp (accessed December 26, 2009).

p. 42, "If I decided to run . . .": Reagan, *An American Life*, 148.

p. 43, "Reagan is only an . . .": Edmund Brown, quoted in Reagan, *An American Life*, 151.

p. 43, "turned out to be . . .": Reagan, *An American Life*, 152.

p. 46, "I knew I had to . . .": Reagan, *An American Life*, 156.

CHAPTER FIVE

p. 50, "Some people have suggested . . .": Reagan, *An American Life*, 162.

p. 52, "When Nixon was nominated . . .": Reagan, *An American Life*, 178.

p. 56, "After Ford's loss . . .": Reagan, *An American Life*, 203–204.

p. 57, "an excellent leader of our . . .": Gerald Ford, quoted in John M. Broder, "Reagan Remembered for Leadership and Optimism," the *New York Times*, June 6, 2004, www.nytimes.com/2004/06/06/us/reagan-remembered-for-leadership-and-optimism.html?pagewanted=1 (accessed December 26, 2009).

p. 57, "probably the least well-informed . . .": Gerald Ford, quoted in Associated Press, "Ford Thought of Carter as a 'Disaster,'" *MSNBC*, January 12, 2007, www.msnbc.msn.com/id/16599540/ns/politics-gerald_r_ford/ (accessed December 27, 2009).

p. 57, "was just a poor manager . . .": Gerald Ford, quoted in Associated Press, "Ford Thought of Carter as a 'Disaster.'"

CHAPTER SIX

p. 61, "It might be well . . .": Ronald Reagan, quoted in John C. Maxwell, *Leadership Gold: Lessons Learned from a Lifetime of Leading* (Nashville: Thomas Nelson, 2008), 75.

p. 67, "I believe that communism . . .": Ronald Reagan, quoted in Paul Kengor, *God and Ronald Reagan: A Spiritual Life* (New York: ReganBooks, 2004), 240.

CHAPTER SEVEN

p. 71, "I will not make age . . .": Ronald Reagan, quoted in Edmund Morris, *Dutch: A Memoir of Ronald Reagan* (New York: Random House, 1999), 506.

p. 73, "When I took this oath . . .": Ronald Reagan, quoted in Associated Press, "Transcript of Reagan's Second Inaugural Address on January 21, 1985," the *Baltimore Sun*, January 21, 1985, www.baltimoresun.com/business/sns-reagan-address1985,0,1055558.story?page=1 (accessed December 27, 2009).

p. 75, "There will be more shuttle . . .": Reagan, *An American Life*, 403.

p. 79, "When our citizens are . . .": Ronald Reagan, quoted in Joe Scarborough, *The Last Best Hope: Restoring Conservatism and America's Promise* (New York: Crown, 2009), 45.

p. 83, "I take full responsibility . . .": Ronald Reagan, *Speaking My Mind: Selected Speeches* (New York: Simon & Schuster, 1989), 399.

CHAPTER EIGHT

p. 86, "General Secretary Gorbachev . . .": Reagan, *Speaking My Mind*, 377.

p. 87, "A true leader . . ." : Mikhail Gorbachev, "A President Who Listened," the *New York Times*, June 7, 2004, www.nytimes.com/2004/06/07/opinion/a-president-who-listened.html?pagewanted=1 (accessed December 27, 2009).

p. 87, "I won a nickname . . .": Ronald Reagan, quoted in Edward M. Yager, *Ronald Reagan's Journey: Democrat to Republican* (Lanham, MD: Rowman & Littlefield, 2006), 113.

p. 90, "I now begin the journey . . .": Ronald Reagan, quoted in Marilyn Berger, "The 40th President: The Life," the *New York Times*, June 7, 2004, www.nytimes.com/2004/06/07/us/40th-president-life-champion-small-government-who-helped-reset-world-stage.html?pagewanted=1 (accessed December 27, 2009).

p. 92, "I know in my heart . . .": Reagan, *Speaking My Mind*, 410.

GLOSSARY

acclaim praise and approval

ayatollah an Islamic leader who is often viewed as both a political and religious authority

blacklist to place people on a list or within a category that removes them from favor

budget deficit an economic situation that occurs when a government or business spends more than it earns

conservative supportive of more traditional political policies and in opposition to those that favor any sort of extreme changes

democracy a system of government that is run by the people or representatives who speak for them

diplomatic related to the relationship between two nations

Electoral College a group of representatives from every state who vote in presidential elections and who are supposed to pick the candidate that the majority of residents in their geographic area consider most popular

extremists individuals with radical or uncompromising views

guerilla related to unconventional methods of armed warfare; guerilla troops typically attack a larger enemy using ambushes, raids, and other forms of harassment

impeached removed from office

legislators lawmakers

liberal supportive of political policies that are typically more rooted in change and progress than traditional ideas and values

moderate mild or not extreme

monopolies markets that feature many buyers or people who need services but only one seller or individual who provides them

primary early election in which voters choose a candidate to represent their geographic area or political party in a later race for a certain office

propaganda information that is purposely spread to promote a certain cause

reforms changes that are intended to improve a situation or policy

regulation control over standards or rules within a business or organization

reserve armed forces that are not on active duty but that can be called to service in emergency situations, such as war

shah the title held by former monarchs of Iran who controlled that country until the late 1970s

subversion acts that are designed to overthrow or destroy an organized government

terrorism the act of using organized violence as a political weapon

union an organization of workers or tradespeople who join together in an effort to protect their rights and interests

warmonger someone who favors war or policies that promote military aggression

Further Information

Books

Brownell, Richard. *The Cold War*. Detroit: Lucent Books, 2009.

Klobuchar, Lisa. *The Iran-Contra Affair: Political Scandal Uncovered*. Minneapolis: Compass Point Books, 2008.

Stewart, James. *Lebanon*. Vero Beach, FL: Rourke Publishing, 2008.

Sutcliffe, Jane. *Ronald Reagan*. Minneapolis: Lerner Publications Company, 2008.

DVD

Ronald Reagan: An American President. DVD. 20th Century Fox, 2005.

Websites

About the White House: Presidents—Ronald Reagan: 1981–1989

www.whitehouse.gov/about/presidents/ronaldreagan

The official White House website details the life and accomplishments of the fortieth president of the United States.

PBS American Experience: Reagan

www.pbs.org/wgbh/amex/reagan/

This website contains a collection of online resources that features a timeline and biographical data on Reagan.

RonaldReagan.com

www.ronaldreagan.com

This website contains speeches and numerous autobiographical accounts provided by Reagan.

Ronald Reagan Presidential Foundation and Library

www.reaganlibrary.com/

This website contains a detailed overview of the library and museum, as well as a series of online documents that deal with Reagan's administration.

BIBLIOGRAPHY

BOOKS

Cannon, Lou. *Governor Reagan: His Rise to Power*. New York: Public Affairs, 2003.

——. *Ronald Reagan: The Presidential Portfolio: A History Illustrated from the Collection of the Ronald Reagan Library and Museum.* New York: Public Affairs, 2001.

Edwards, Lee. *The Essential Ronald Reagan: A Profile in Courage, Justice, and Wisdom.* Lanham, MD: Rowman & Littlefield, 2004.

Friedenberg, Robert V. *Notable Speeches in Contemporary Presidential Campaigns.* Westport, CT: Praeger, 2002.

Kengor, Paul. *God and Ronald Reagan: A Spiritual Life.* New York: ReganBooks, 2004.

Maxwell, John C. *Leadership Gold: Lessons Learned from a Lifetime of Leading.* Nashville: Thomas Nelson, 2008.

Morris, Edmund. *Dutch: A Memoir of Ronald Reagan.* New York: Random House, 1999.

Reagan, Ronald. *An American Life.* New York: Simon & Schuster, 1990.

——. *Speaking My Mind: Selected Speeches.* New York: Simon & Schuster, 1989.

Scarborough, Joe. *The Last Best Hope: Restoring Conservatism and America's Promise.* New York: Crown, 2009.

Yager, Edward M. *Ronald Reagan's Journey: Democrat to Republican.* Lanham, MD: Rowman & Littlefield, 2006.

DVD

Ronald Reagan: An American President. DVD. 20th Century Fox, 2005.

Online Articles

The Associated Press. "Ford Thought of Carter as a 'Disaster,'"
MSNBC, January 12, 2007. www.msnbc.msn.com/id/16599540/ns/
politics-gerald_r_ford/ (accessed December 27, 2009).

——. "Transcript of Reagan's Second Inaugural Address on January 21,
1985," *Baltimore Sun*, January 21, 1985. www.baltimoresun.com/
business/sns-reagan-address1985,0,1055558.story?page=1
(accessed December 27, 2009).

Berger, Marilyn. "The 40th President: The Life," the *New York Times*,
June 7, 2004. www.nytimes.com/2004/06/07/us/40th-president-life-
champion-small-government-who-helped-reset-world-stage.
html?pagewanted=1 (accessed December 27, 2009).

Broder, John M. "Reagan Remembered for Leadership and Optimism,"
the *New York Times*, June 6, 2004. www.nytimes.com/2004/06/06/
us/reagan-remembered-for-leadership-and-optimism.html?pagewant
ed=1 (accessed December 26, 2009).

The Federal Bureau of Investigation. "Remarks by Robert S. Mueller, III,
    Director, Federal Bureau of Investigation, InfraGard 2005 National
    Conference, Washington, D.C., August 9, 2005," *The Federal
    Bureau of Investigation Major Executive Speeches*, August 9, 2005.
    www.fbi.gov/pressrel/speeches/mueller080905.htm (accessed
    December 27, 2009).

Gorbachev, Mikhail. "A President Who Listened," the *New York Times*,
    June 7, 2004. www.associatedcontent.com/article/415589/ronald_
    reagan_the_most_successful_actor.html (accessed January 21, 2009)

Hopwood, Jon C. "Ronald Reagan: The Most Successful Actor in World
    History," *Associated Content*, October 15, 2007. www.newsweek.
    com/id/172561 (accessed December 26, 2009).

Rosenblatt, Roger. "1980: Ronald Reagan," *TIME*, January 2, 1981.
    www.time.com/time/subscriber/personoftheyear/archive/
    stories/1980.html (accessed December 26, 2009).

Whitney, Gleaves. "Ronald Reagan, R.I.P.," the *National Review*,
    January 7, 2004. www.nationalreview.com/comment/
    whitney200406070843.asp (accessed December 26, 2009).

Additional Web Resources That Were Not Quoted

About the White House: Presidents—Ronald Reagan: 1981–1989

www.whitehouse.gov/about/presidents/ronaldreagan

Dave Leip's Atlas of U.S. Presidential Elections

http://uselectionatlas.org

PBS American Experience: Reagan

www.pbs.org/wgbh/amex/reagan/

RonaldReagan.com

www.ronaldreagan.com

The Ronald Reagan Presidential Foundation and Library

www.reaganlibrary.com

United States Department of Labor: Bureau of Labor Statistics

www.bls.gov/CPI

INDEX

Pages in **boldface** are illustrations.

abortion, position on, 49
acting career, **20**, **22**
    education and, 11, 13
    film career, 18–22, 25
    public speaking and, 43
    television roles, 35
    World War II and, 27, 28
age, Reagan's, 60, 71
Agnew, Spiro, 54
Alzheimer's disease, 90
An American Life (Reagan), 88
arms for hostages deals, 79–83
Army service, World War II and, 26–28
assassination attempt, 66
autobiography, 88

Beirut Marine barracks, bombing of, 68–69, **69**
Berlin Wall, **86**, 86
blacklisting, 31–32
Boland Amendments, 81, 83
Brown, Edmund "Pat," 41, **42**, 43, 45
budget deficits, 45–46, 47, 65
Bush, George H. W., 60, **61**, 87, **89**, 89
business regulation, 35, 36, 64

California Welfare Reform Act (CWRA) (1971), 52
Carter, James "Jimmy," 55, 56, 89, **89**
Challenger space shuttle, 75, **76**
childhood, 8, **9**, 10–12
children, 22, **27**, 28, 32
cold war
    communism and, 29–30
    Mikhail Gorbachev and, 73–74
    military spending and, 65, 67
    Reagan's legacy and, 91
    second presidential term and, 84–85, 86, 87
college years, 12–14
communism, 29–31, 31–32, 44, 67, 69–70
    See also Soviet Union
Congress, U.S., 30–32

conservative politics, 37, 55, 60, 91
Contras, Nicaragua and, 81

Davis, Nancy. *See* Reagan, Nancy
death, of Ronald Reagan, 91
Democratic Party, 36
divorce, 28
drugs, war on, 74–75
Dukakis, Michael, 87

economic issues, 7, 36, 38, 71
    first presidential term and, 62–65
    Jimmy Carter and, 58
    Reagan's legacy and, 91
    Soviet Union and, 84–85
Economic Recovery Tax Act (ERTA) (1981), 64
education, 11–12, 12–14
elections
    election of 1964, 38, 41
    election of 1968, 50–52
    election of 1976, 54–56
    election of 1980, 58–60, 62
    election of 1984, 71, 73
    election of 1988, 87
for governor of California, 41–45, 50
employment
    acting career, 18–22, 25
    the Great Depression and, 14–15
    high school and college, 10, 11, 12, 13
    radio career, 16–17

Ford, Gerald, **54**, **56**, 89, **89**
    election of 1976, 55, 56
    opinion of Reagan and, 57
    presidency and, 53–54
foreign policy
    election of 1984 and, 71
    first presidential term and, 65, 67–70
    Jimmy Carter and, 58–59
    Reagan's legacy and, 7, 8, 91
    second presidential term and, 73–74, 76–83, 84–85, 86, 87

Al-Gadhafi, Mu'ammar, **77**, 77–78
General Electric Theater, 35, 37
Goldwater, Barry, 38, **39**, 41, 51
Gorbachev, Mikhail, 73–74, **74**, 84, 85, 86, 87
governing style, Reagan and, 7–8, 49–50, 57, 73
governor, of California, 41–45, 45–46, 47, 49–50
grave, inscription on, 92
Great Communicator, nickname, 7, 87
Great Depression, 14–15, 19
Grenada, invasion of, 69–70, **70**

Hezbollah, 68, 69, 79–80
high school years, **11**, 11–12, **12**
hijackings, 76–77
Hinckley, John, Jr., 66
hostage-taking, 58–59, 62, 79–81, 82–83
House Committee on Un-American Activities, 30–31, **31**, 31–32

impeachment, Richard Nixon and, 53
inflation, 58, 62–63, 64
Iran-Contra affair, 80, 81–83
Iranian hostage crisis, 58–59, 62
Israel, 80

Johnson, Lyndon B., 38, 41

Kennedy, John F., 36
Khomeini, Ayatollah, 58, 80
Knute Rockne — All American (film), 22, **24**, 25

Lebanon, 68–69, 76–77, 79–80
legacy, of Ronald Reagan, 91–92
legislature, working with, 47, 49
Libya, 77–79, **78**
loyalty oaths, 30–31

marriages, 22, 28, 32, **33**
McAuliffe, Christa, 75
Middle East, foreign policy and, 8, 58–59, 62, 68–69, 77–79, 79–81
military actions, 68–69, 69–70, **70**, 78–79
military spending, 65, 67–68, 84

missile shield project (Strategic Defense Initiative), 67–68
Mondale, Walter, 71, **72**

Nicaragua, 81–83
nicknames, 7, 10
Nixon, Richard, 36, 50–52, **51**, 52–53, **53**, **89**, 89
North, Oliver, 81, 82, **82**
nuclear weapons, 85

Poindexter, John, 81, 82
political career
  college years and, 14
  first presidential term and, 66, 67–70
  governor of California, 45–46, 47, 49–50, 52
  Screen Actors Guild (SAG) and, 28–29
  second presidential term and, 73–83, 84–85, 86
  See also elections
political cartoons, **30**, **53**
post-war era, communism and, 29–32
presidency
  first presidential term and, 66, 67–70
  Jimmy Carter and, 58–60, 62
  second presidential term and, 73–83, 84–85, 86
  See also elections
public opinion, of Reagan, 83
public speaking
  college years, 14
  election campaigns and, 38, 41, 43, 45, 55, 60, 62
  political issues and, 35, 37, 86
  presidency and, 75, 87

radio career, 16–17, 18, **18**, 20
Reagan, John Edward "Jack," 8, **9**, 10, 19
Reagan, Maureen Elizabeth, 22, **27**
Reagan, Michael Edward, 28
Reagan, Nancy, 32, **33**, 34, 42, **88**, 88, 90
Reagan, Neil, 8, **9**, 10, 19
Reagan, Nelle Wilson, 8, **9**, 10, 19
Reagan, Patricia Ann "Patti," 32
Reagan, Ronald
  childhood, 8, **9**, 10–12, **11**

children, 22, **27**, 28, 32
death of, 91
marriages, 22, 28, 32, **33**
parents and, 19
retirement, 87–90, **88**, **89**
Reagan, Ronald Prescott (son), 32
Reaganomics, 62–65
recession (1981 to 1982), 65
religious beliefs, 10
Republican Party, 36–37, 38, 41
retirement, 87–90
Ronald W. Reagan Presidential Library and Museum, **89**, 89
Russian Federation, 85, 87

Screen Actors Guild (SAG), 28–29
Soviet Union
    election of 1980 and, 60
    first presidential term and, 65, 67
    post-war era and, 29–30
    second presidential term and, 73–74, 84–85, 86, 87
space shuttle disaster, 75
sports broadcasting, 16–17, **18**
Strategic Defense Initiative (SDI), 67–68

taxes, 45–46, 47, 64
television roles, 35, 37
terrorism, 7, 76–77, 78, 79–83, 91
Therapeutic Abortion Act (1967), 49
Timeline, 94–95
Tower Commission, 81–82

unemployment, 63, 64, 65

Vietnam War, 38, 44

Warner Brothers, 19–20, 20–21, 27
Watergate scandal, 52–53
welfare reforms, 52
World War II, 26–28
Wyman, Jane, 21, 22, **23**, **27**, 28

ABOUT THE AUTHOR

Katie Marsico is the author of more than sixty reference books for children and young adults. Prior to becoming a full-time writer, Marsico worked as a managing editor in publishing. She resides near Chicago, Illinois, with her husband, daughter, and two sons.